5⁰⁰

How I Learned
Soul Travel

How I Learned Soul Travel

Terrill Willson

The True Experiences of a Student in
ECKANKAR, the Ancient Science of Soul Travel

Illuminated Way Publishing
P.O. Box 28130 • Crystal, Minnesota 55428

How I Learned Soul Travel

Copyright © 1987 Terrill Willson

Printed in U.S.A.

ISBN: 0-88155-052-3

Library of Congress Catalog Card Number: 87-081288

Edited by Mary Carroll and Joan Klemp

Cover design by Lois Stanfield

Contents

1

What This Book's About

Several years ago something unusual happened to me: I experienced a form of physical death and lived to tell the tale. With full consciousness, and of my own free will, I moved out of my physical body and returned to it again a short time later.

I had never heard of the possibility of out-of-body travel. My thoughts about life revolved solely around the physical world. But after this startling experience, my thinking had to be expanded to include the possibility of life beyond the physical realm.

Very intrigued by what had happened to me, I tried to reexperience this same phenomenon during the days that followed. Eventually, I succeeded. My second out-of-body experience turned out quite different from my first, and my curiosity kept me trying to learn and understand more.

This book is a journey through the past several years of my life, focusing specifically on how I came in contact with the idea of Soul Travel. I've slowly progressed in being able to consciously leave my body, and I've learned about the existence of nonphysical worlds.

Written or spoken words can't fully convince people of these realities, but my succession of experiences may spark your interest to the possibility of Soul Travel. You may even achieve your own first conscious out-of-body experience through the different techniques described. At the very least you may find Soul Travel interesting.

Here's my story.

2

A High Whistle

I 'm a single fellow in my early thirties. I grew up in a large family in a medium-sized town in the midwest and have always been somewhat of a loner. I was never much of a socialite, or a particularly popular person throughout school. In most respects I'm pretty average, although I'm intelligent and have good common sense.

After graduating from college, the idea of an eight-to-five job didn't appeal to me. I worked in construction a few years, saved my money, and bought a used motor home. Fixing up the motor home took a number of months, but finally I packed all my belongings and drove off, heading for new horizons. This is how I've lived for the past seven years, carving a wandering trail through the United States and parts of southern Canada.

To support myself I work about four to six months each year on riverboats. We push barges up and down the Mississippi, Ohio, and Illinois rivers. Although the work isn't that enjoyable, I am able to save some money and keep a flexible living and traveling schedule. For now, the job suits me and fits my lifestyle. When I don't work, I can travel, going where I want and doing as I please. I've seen and done and learned many things as well during these traveling years. I honestly believe that had I not chosen this rather unusual

3

lifestyle after college, I probably would never have taken the time to discover the reality of Soul Travel.

In spite of priding myself on being an independent person, in the first few months of traveling I felt terribly alone. As time passed, though, I started enjoying my new life of freedom. It was at about this time I began to do some serious soul-searching. I started asking myself the age-old questions: Who I was? What made me tick? How could I become a better person? I was searching for something, something about myself or something about life. With plenty of free time for thinking, I became interested in how my mind worked. What caused me to be the kind of person I was? Could I control my mind and initiate positive changes within myself?

Trying to improve my attitude toward life and other people prompted me to begin reading about positive thinking. Before long, I was enthusiastically trying to apply these principles to my everyday thoughts. But gradually it became obvious that the benefits of positive thinking were only temporary, at least for me. It was a source of mental strength and upliftment for awhile, and it opened up my mind to ideas and opinions that I'd previously considered invalid. My views concerning life, religion, psychic phenomena, and philosophical matters had always been fairly rigid and conservative. Positive thinking pushed me in the direction of considering and respecting other people's views and opinions which differed from my own. But that was its only lasting effect.

Next I entered a phase of self-examination and self-criticism. Still trying to improve myself, I started analyzing my daily thoughts and actions, judging them for their good or bad qualities. I soon realized how terribly destructive to character and confidence this can be. Constant self-analysis and self-criticism can quickly make an unhappy person out of anyone. I wasted no time in putting a halt to this.

I was still learning, and my next mental experiment was meditation. I had heard that it was supposed to be beneficial in some way, so I bought several books on the subject and curiously started reading. After finishing the books, I still didn't really understand what meditation was or how it was supposed to be helpful. But the idea of meditating intrigued me, so I decided to give it a try.

I started meditating each day for twenty minutes or so in the manner described in one of the books. Surprisingly, within just a matter of days, changes started showing up in my personality and behavior. They seemed to be good changes, surfacing from deep within me. I couldn't consciously take credit for causing them or bringing them about, but somehow these short daily meditations were helping me to be less reactive and more calm and relaxed.

Seeing these positive changes in my emotional behavior gave me the incentive to continue meditating daily for the next six to eight months. How or why meditation worked remained a mystery to me, but I gradually became a less reactive, more relaxed and confident, and better-communicating person.

Two details concerning meditation later paid dividends when I came in contact with the idea of Soul Travel. One of the meditation books made reference to the term *Spiritual Eye,* which I'd never heard of before. Although I didn't really understand or pay much attention to why the *Spiritual Eye* was important, reading about and remembering this term later proved valuable to me.

I also began hearing a faint high whistle in the top of my head. As the weeks and months passed, this sound gradually became louder and easier for me to hear during my meditation sessions. I didn't find out until many months later that this sound was a first step to Soul Travel.

3

Two Books about Soul Travel

A bout seven months later, I happened to make the acquaintance of a young man while working on a riverboat. Both of us worked the same shift and we had both brought along several books to read in our spare time. One day I glanced at two of his books. They were entitled *In My Soul I Am Free* by Brad Steiger and *ECKANKAR—The Key to Secret Worlds* by Paul Twitchell. I looked at them curiously and asked my friend what they were about. His brief explanation about a spiritual path called Eckankar didn't mean much to me, but when he mentioned the term *Spiritual Eye,* my attention perked up. I remembered these words. I proudly announced that I, too, had heard of the Spiritual Eye from my involvement with meditation. Our conversation continued along the lines of meditation and spiritual matters, and I finally asked the fellow if I could read his books.

Several days later I skimmed through the book *ECKANKAR—The Key to Secret Worlds,* to get an idea of what it was about. Only a few chapters caught my interest, though; the contents seemed too far out to believe! The book was spiritually-oriented and was based on an idea I'd never heard of, that of out-of-body travel. Although the idea of being able to consciously leave the physical body sounded interesting, it also seemed rather unrealistic and hard to believe. I also wondered how it could possibly apply to me. So I set the book aside with no further intentions of reading it again.

A day or so later I leafed through the other book *In My Soul I Am Free*. This book looked a little more interesting to me. I began reading more slowly through it. When I finished the book, I could hardly believe what I'd just read. I immediately went back and read it again, being just as fascinated the second time through as the first. The book seemed to be written in a truthful, matter-of-fact way, yet what was said was so incredible.

In My Soul I Am Free is about a man named Paul Twitchell. He was said to have developed the ability to consciously leave his physical body at will and project instantly to any place in any world he wanted to. He reportedly learned how to consciously leave his physical body at a very young age from his sister and father and became very adept at this as he grew older.

In spite of never before having heard of this unusual idea of out-of-body travel, the unbiased, documentary tone of *In My Soul I Am Free* actually led me to believe that maybe Paul Twitchell did have this ability. Astounded by this possibility, I immediately went back and reread Paul Twitchell's book *ECKANKAR—The Key to Secret Worlds*, this time more slowly and with a great deal more interest. After finishing the book, I could again hardly believe what I'd just read. This book, too, sounded truthfully written now that out-of-body travel seemed a little more believable to me.

Reading these two books had the effect of putting me in a mild state of shock. Not only could Paul Twitchell consciously leave his physical body at will, but both books suggested that this is something anyone could learn how to do. Claims were made that many, many people throughout the world consciously project out of the body every day.

I couldn't help feeling somewhat excited about what this meant. As Mr. Twitchell broadly put it in his book: Being able to consciously leave the physical body is a latent ability within each and every person. This meant that I, Terrill Willson, could consciously experience and verify something as incredible as leaving my physical body and traveling to other places on earth in a so-called Soul body or spirit body. This Soul body would consist of high vibration and energy rather than physical substance and therefore be invisible to human eyes. In the Soul body I would be able to think conscious thoughts, feel emotions, and have all the senses of touch, taste, smell, hearing, and sight.

It sounded so fantastic that I wondered if it could really be true. Why hadn't I heard of anything like this before? If people really could consciously leave their bodies, why wasn't there more talk about it? I was excited and curious, amazed and doubtful. I honestly didn't know what to think at this point or how far to open my mind to this new idea of out-of-body travel.

Paul Twitchell's book *ECKANKAR—The Key to Secret Worlds* spoke of many spiritual concepts much loftier than the idea of out-of-body travel, concepts such as Spirit and Soul and God and inner worlds and inner Godmen. But the only part of the book that interested me was the discussion about moving out of body to other places on earth. The accounts and descriptions given in the book of famous and non-famous people who'd become adept at out-of-body travel were especially interesting to me. There were also several techniques described for interested beginners.

One could project out of body either in the physical environment or move into inner worlds which Mr. Twitchell claimed exist. These inner worlds, or inner planes, were described as being just as solid and real as the physical world but were made up of higher vibration and energy. Talk of these inner worlds didn't mean much to me, though. These inner worlds and other lofty spiritual concepts didn't seem tangible or real to me. I could really relate to the idea of consciously leaving my body to travel to other places on earth, moving in an inner body that looked and felt like my physical form; this was something I could picture in my mind and even more importantly something that supposedly anyone, even I, could consciously experience and learn to do.

After rereading *ECKANKAR — The Key to Secret Worlds* a second time, I knew I would have to give out-of-body travel a try. My efforts might not be successful, but my desire to try was strong, natural, and compelling, rooted deep inside me. I felt driven to give Soul Travel a good, honest attempt. This would surely be the ultimate in excitement and adventure.

4

Soul Travel Technique

I wanted to try moving out of the body right away but didn't have the opportunity until about a week later. The poor living conditions on the riverboat and the unusual and tiring work-sleep schedule of six hours on, six hours off, seven days a week, made it difficult to get enough rest. Finally, one sleep period I decided it was time to try to leave my body. Anxious to see if any of the techniques listed in the book *ECKANKAR—The Key to Secret Worlds* would work for me, I carefully read through the several described and decided to try the first one.

The book describes this particular technique as follows. Upon going to bed, I was to relax and imagine myself in some specific location outside my physical body. While focusing my thoughts like this, I was supposed to stay as relaxed as possible and allow myself to gradually fall asleep. The location didn't matter, but in order to be successful, my desire to travel to this place would have to be strong.

According to Mr. Twitchell's book, when Soul is separated from the physical body, It moves from one location to another by thought. If I found myself drifting into sleep and then suddenly became aware that I was hovering above my physical body, by recognizing the situation calmly and thinking of where I'd previously wanted to travel to, I would instantly find myself in that location.

I decided to try to imagine myself being inside my motor home. My motor home seemed like the most logical place to try, because I could clearly imagine what the inside looked like. I closed my eyes and began trying to visualize the interior in detail. I also tried to imagine myself being there, and even tried imagining myself touching things like the walls and the bed and the table.

It soon became obvious that trying to focus my thoughts and my attention like this was much more difficult than I'd expected. In spite of being very familiar with the inside of my motor home I couldn't seem to hold a clear mental picture of what it looked like, even for a few seconds. Each time I tried, my mind would quickly jump to some other unrelated thought. It was almost as if my conscious mind was afraid to let me reach a high level of concentration.

No matter how hard I tried or how much will power I attempted to generate, I simply couldn't concentrate my thoughts even for a few seconds. It soon became very frustrating as well as mentally and physically tiring. Whenever I did get relatively close to reaching a high level of concentration, my mind would again wander off, forcing me to retrieve it and start over again. After awhile it became obvious that I wasn't the master of my own mind; in fact, my conscious mind seemed to be developing a mind of its own.

I didn't understand until months later that forced concentration like this is very difficult for most people. Ordinarily the conscious mind is accustomed to the habit of moving constantly from one thought to another. I learned during the following months that this habit isn't easily broken; trying to lock the conscious mind onto one single thought or picture for any length of time sounds much easier to do than it actually is.

My only encouragement during this first hour and a half of failing miserably was hearing that familiar, faint high whistle in the top of my head. This was the same sound spoken of in Paul Twitchell's book and the one I'd heard countless times before during my meditation sessions. I couldn't recall what Paul Twitchell had said about it or why it was supposed to be important, except that it had something to do with Soul Travel. But it didn't seem to be helping me leave my body, which was all I cared about at that moment.

If my desire to move out of the body hadn't been so strong, I probably would have given up at this point and just gone to sleep. But I still wanted to believe that maybe I could somehow do it, so I decided to continue concentrating awhile longer. Then it occurred to me that maybe one of the other out-of-body techniques mentioned in Paul Twitchell's book would be easier.

Since the room I was sleeping in wasn't totally dark, I tried shifting my attention to a spot at the center of the ceiling to establish a downward 360 degree view of everything in the room from this overhead vantage point. I soon found this kind of concentration just as difficult and tiring for me as trying to visualize the inside of my motor home. My mind still wandered continually to unrelated thoughts. After thirty or forty-five minutes of trying unsuccessfully to concentrate in this manner, I changed tactics again and tried another technique. Now I tried to imagine myself floating weightlessly around the room. At the same time I tried to see everything in the room in detail, but my ability to concentrate didn't improve. Regardless of what I tried to mentally visualize, no amount of willpower or determination could hold my mind to one picture or one idea.

I spent a total of three long, futile, frustrating hours that night. In dire need of sleep before having to go back to work again, I was about to give up. Then something happened that caught me by complete surprise—something I didn't even know was possible.

One moment I was wide awake both mentally and physically, discouraged and frustrated and feeling very, very tired. The next moment I was still wideawake mentally, but sound asleep physically. I didn't feel anything unusual when this happened. Just all of a sudden, I noticed my physical body had fallen asleep.

This strange sensation wasn't frightening. Mentally I was in complete control of the situation and knew exactly what was happening. I vaguely remembered something like this being discussed somewhere in Paul Twitchell's book, possibly happening just prior to moving out of body. As the seconds passed, this sleeping/waking situation became more and more exciting. For some reason, I now felt much closer to being able to leave my body. My thoughts were much clearer, and concentration seemed much easier for me than before.

To keep from waking my physical body and ruining this neat sleeping/waking state, I remained perfectly motionless. I tried to figure out how to take advantage of this possible Soul Travel opportunity, but unfortunately, couldn't think of what to do next. A short time later I slipped into sleep. The next thing I knew, I was waking up a couple of hours later to go to work.

5

A Little Success

E ach day for the next week or so, I tried concentrating very hard for a couple of hours on moving out of my body, but without success. I couldn't even duplicate the phenomenon of falling asleep physically yet remaining awake mentally. I was tired and frustrated with my failures, but my desire to try to move out of body still remained strong. Having experienced the exciting and unusual sleeping/waking state, I still wanted to believe that out-of-body travel was possible. I kept trying, thinking that sooner or later my ability to concentrate would begin to improve.

All this time, strangely enough, I was still hearing the faint high whistle inside my head. Each time I started concentrating, it wasn't long before it became clearly audible. My curiosity as to what this sound meant prompted me to search through the book *ECKANKAR—The Key to Secret Worlds* for an answer.

In his book Paul Twitchell stated that this faint high whistle is a vital ingredient of Spirit, which emanates directly from God. God is an immense ocean of Light and Sound, and flowing from God is a mammoth wave of this Light and Sound, called Spirit. Spirit is the source of energy from which all physical and nonphysical forms are made, a powerful current having innate intelligence. It gives the spark of life and sustains the spark of life in all Souls and life forms everywhere. According to Mr. Twitchell, this wave of Spirit flowing outward from God eventually returns again to God, in a ceaseless, eternal, circular flow.

Paul Twitchell claimed that this Sound Current is the carrier and mode of transportation used for transcending the physical body. Soul Traveling to other places in the physical world, or into any of the inner worlds, is supposedly accomplished by actually riding this current of Sound out of the physical body. This sound is audible to the inner ears as a faint high whistle and can be heard differently in each of the inner worlds. Variations on this inner Sound include thunder, the roar of the sea, the tinkling of bells, running water, buzzing of bees, the single note of a flute, a heavy wind, deep humming, a thousand violins, the music of woodwinds, the sound of a whirlpool, and others.

Paul Twitchell's lengthy explanation about this Sound Current was new and interesting information, but hard for me to get excited about. My main interest centered on the possibility of out-of-body travel, not spiritual ideas. Since this faint high whistle didn't seem to be helpful during my concentration attempts, I didn't pay much attention to the importance Mr. Twitchell credited this sound with.

My primary concern at this point was my obvious inability to fully and properly concentrate. It seemed logical to assume that if out-of-body travel was for real, then concentration would have to be my ticket to success. Therefore, my thoughts and my enthusiasm about the possibility of Soul Travel turned toward somehow improving my concentration ability, and the only way I could think of to do this was through practice.

My plan of attack was to continue my concentration efforts whenever convenient for me, with the hopes of gradually improving my level of concentration. By doing this, maybe I could achieve that first conscious out-of-body experience, preferably in the not-too-distant future. Maybe more out-of-body experiences would then follow.

16

In spite of not even being certain as to the reality of out-of-body travel, I still couldn't help thinking how incredibly exciting it would be to someday develop the ability to consciously leave my body at will.

6

My First Conscious
Out-of-Body Experience

Then it happened—my first conscious out-of-body experience. It was far different from what I expected, but it was still very real and very exciting. Only a few weeks earlier I wouldn't have dreamed something like this could be possible.

I was still working on a riverboat at the time. It was a couple of weeks after I'd read *In My Soul I Am Free* and *ECKANKAR—The Key to Secret Worlds*. This particular sleep period I went to bed and began concentrating in the same general manner as I'd been doing for the past week. I was trying to picture some place in my mind in detail and, with great difficulty, to imagine myself actually being there. Changing mental pictures several times didn't help, but I kept trying. After a couple of hours of determined mental effort, fatigue started setting in.

Then something unexpected happened. I suddenly realized that my physical body had fallen asleep, but I was still awake. I immediately recognized this as the same sleeping/waking phenomenon I'd experienced about a week earlier. Startled and excited by this discovery, but careful to remain absolutely motionless and calm in order not to wake my

19

physical body, I pondered what to do next. I was unable to recall Paul Twitchell's book mentioning any specific suggestions for this kind of situation, so for lack of knowing what else to do, I decided to try leaving my physical body through the top of my head.

Paul Twitchell had said in his book that the two best places for Soul to leave the physical body were the Spiritual Eye (located at the base of the nose between the eyebrows) and the top of the head. I began to imagine myself moving weightlessly out through the top of my head, placing my thoughts several feet above me. With the physical body asleep, it was much easier to focus my thoughts and reach a high level of concentration.

After maybe a minute of trying to focus my thoughts in this manner, something else happened. The faint high whistle, which had been audible all along in the top of my head, shifted to my right ear and started getting louder. Remembering that Paul Twitchell had said that just prior to leaving the body, a loud roar might possibly develop in the right ear, I continued imagining myself moving weightlessly out through the top of my head. The whistle in my right ear quickly developed into an extremely loud roar. I honestly thought my right eardrum might break!

Suddenly, the loud roar stopped. I found myself observing from a location above my physical head. Somehow I'd shifted to the place just above the crown of my head, where moments before I'd been trying to place my thoughts.

Fully conscious before, during, and after this out-of-body movement, I now found myself in a world of blackness which was dotted with many distant tiny white specks of light. They looked like stars in outer space. Surprisingly, I felt no fear in this situation. The movement had happened so quickly and so unexpectedly that I actually didn't have time to feel any fear. One moment I was worried about my right eardrum possibly rupturing, and the next moment the loud roar had stopped as I found myself outside my physical body, enveloped in a world of starry darkness.

Perhaps my biggest surprise was that I now had no body form at all! From my position just a few feet above my physical head, I could think conscious thoughts and feel emotions, yet I amazingly had no detectable body form. I was still me, Terrill Willson, but as far as I could tell I consisted of nothing more than a bodiless unit of awareness.

Added to this was another amazing reality—my mental capacity was now a hundred or a thousand times more acute than normal! I began hearing conversations between other people, three separate conversations coming from different directions in the surrounding darkness. The voices sounded quite close to me, each coming from within ten or fifteen feet. Two of the conversations were between a man and a woman and the third involved a crying baby.

The moment after moving out of my body, I realized that there was a problem with my sleeping physical form. It had rolled toward the open side of the top bunk bed. I could somehow tell that it had slumped over and now lay dangerously perched on the open edge, close to falling onto the floor about five feet below. The situation was serious but stable. Lying balanced on the open edge of the top bunk bed, my physical form had stopped rolling and was now stationary. There was time for a few seconds of deliberation. I decided that my only option was to return to my body and move it to a safe position on the bed. After doing this, I would try to leave the body again.

I didn't really want to return to my physical body. I'd put forth so many long and difficult hours of concentration during the past week just to leave it, but under the circumstances I knew it was necessary to go back. It was logical to assume that I should be able to leave my body a second time, since I'd moved out of it once and ought to be able to do it again.

Getting back inside my physical body was easy; I just imagined the physical senses returning and suddenly found myself feeling my physical arms and legs again. For a short time I continued lying perfectly motionless on the open edge of the bunk bed in this delicate sleeping/waking state, marveling at what I'd just experienced. Back within the confines of my physical body, however, I noticed with disappointment that my mental abilities were no longer impressive. My thinking was now limited to that of my everyday conscious mind, and along with this tremendous decrease in mental powers, I suddenly realized that now many of the details of the out-of-body experience were gone from my memory.

There was also the interesting question of time. While separated from my physical body, time had no meaning. I could only estimate the time-span of the experience. Fifteen seconds or thereabouts seemed a reasonable guess as to how long I'd been out of the body. As for wondering about how much longer I could have remained out, this was something I could only speculate on.

Feeling excited, awed, and somewhat stunned at having achieved this conscious shift out of the body, I was also disappointed about my forced premature return and the accompanying drastic decline in both my mental and memory capabilities. I still assumed that by diligently concentrating in the same manner as before, I ought to be able to move out of my body again. So the first order of business was to roll myself over to a safe and comfortable position in bed. Unfortunately, moving my body caused me to wake up physically as well as mentally, and when I started concentrating again I couldn't seem to properly focus my thoughts.

Finally, after maybe twenty minutes of trying as best I could to concentrate, and feeling very, very tired by this time, I gave up my mental efforts and just went to sleep.

7

Disappointment and Confusion

Without a doubt this fifteen-second experience was the most important event in my life that I could recall. I now had positive, conscious proof that it is possible to leave the physical body and that life does exist beyond this physical world. Admittedly, there wasn't much else about this adventure that I understood or that made much sense to me. But gaining proof that I consist of something more than just a physical form was priceless information to me. As a result, my thinking and my view of life had suddenly changed radically.

All the next day, I was thinking about what I'd experienced and what this first conscious movement out of my body meant to me. My initial impulse was to tell some of the other fellows on the riverboat, and especially the young man whose books I'd borrowed. But who would believe or be able to relate to such a story? I started asking myself how I was going to convince others of my having projected outside my physical body into a vast, timeless world of blackness with no body form. Rather than have people laugh at me or question my mental stability, I reluctantly resigned myself to silence and went back to the reading material to try to find some answers as to what had happened.

23

The most confusing thing about this experience was having no body form at all. Without question, I'd been separated from my physical body. But I had not had any kind of body resembling my physical appearance, so what happened? How could this be? The accounts I remembered from the two books of other people's out-of-body adventures didn't fit at all with this experience of mine. The book descriptions told of other people traveling in a body consisting of high vibrational energy, having the same visible appearance as the physical form.

To try to shed some light on this mystery, I went back and carefully reread parts of *ECKANKAR—The Key to Secret Worlds*. There I found a possible explanation that I'd previously overlooked.

In his book, Paul Twitchell made the rather incredible claim that one can transcend the physical body in the true bodiless Soul form and experience this phenomenon with some degree of consciousness. According to Mr. Twitchell, the real me, the real Terrill Willson, is neither physical body nor conscious mind, but actually a unit of awareness called Soul. Soul is a *personalized* atom of God, capable of knowing all, seeing all, and being everywhere at the same time.

Taking his discussion further than this, Mr. Twitchell gave reasons for each person (Soul) having an outer physical body, plus several different inner bodies. He also discussed a wide variety of other related spiritual concepts, such as what the physical and inner worlds are all about, etc. Then he added weight to these claims by saying that all people are capable of using Soul Travel to consciously verify these statements of his, including experiencing with some degree of consciousness the true bodiless Soul form.

After carefully reading through all this information offered in Mr. Twitchell's book the only thing I could think was that maybe I had been in my true bodiless Soul form. His description of Soul being a bodiless unit of awareness

24

with tremendous thought capability did seem to fit closely with my experience.

8

The Second Out-of-Body Experience

My next opportune sleep period came the following afternoon. Anxiously I lay down in bed and started concentrating again in the same manner as before. But an hour and a half of difficult and tiring effort produced nothing. Other than hearing the faint high whistle in the top of my head, nothing out of the ordinary happened.

Disappointed but not discouraged, I tried concentrating periodically during the next two to three weeks I was working on the riverboat. I continued these hopeful bedtime attempts whenever it was convenient for me. Although I sacrificed a lot of valuable sleep and mental energy in the process, my mental efforts went unrewarded.

I still looked on concentration as the key to Soul Travel success, assuming all along that daily practice would gradually improve my ability to focus my thoughts. But so far this wasn't happening. It seemed clear to me that without a significant improvement in my concentration ability, there wasn't much chance of me ever becoming an accomplished Soul Traveler or, for that matter, even achieving a second out-of-body experience. By this time my enthusiasm and optimism were beginning to suffer. The prospects for future Soul Travel success were looking dim.

Then came that oh-so-important second out-of-body experience, instantly rejuvenating my faltering enthusiasm.

One evening, about five weeks after my first conscious out-of-body experience, I was visiting my brother in the midwest. I had decided at bedtime to try very hard to concentrate and hopefully leave my body. My desire to succeed was especially strong that night as I lay down in bed, closed my eyes, and began looking steadily at the black inner screen in the direction of the Spiritual Eye. This was another Soul Travel technique mentioned in the reading material.

The Spiritual Eye was described in *ECKANKAR—The Key to Secret Worlds* as being one of several locations within the physical form where Soul can leave the physical body. It is located between the eyes at the base of the nose. The black inner screen, sometimes referred to as the inner screen or inner mind screen, is the screen of blackness, sometimes filled with tiny white specks of light, that can easily be seen by closing the eyes and looking straight ahead with the inner vision.

My intentions were to focus my inner gaze on the black inner screen of the Spiritual Eye, until something happened.

After concentrating for maybe thirty minutes with no success, I drifted into sleep, and just at that moment something unusual happened. I caught a brief glimpse of a pattern of rectangles and lights on the black inner screen. This brief moment of consciousness caused me to wake up mentally, even though my physical body had slipped into sleep. Here again was the sleeping/waking phenomenon I'd experienced twice before.

Fully conscious now, I was surprised and very excited at finding myself in this state. Being sure to remain motionless so as not to wake my physical body, my immediate attention went to the strange pattern of lights on my inner mind screen. Somehow a distant pattern of small symmetrical rectangles had formed, about fifteen rows high and twenty rows wide. They were set against a black background and bordered with thin, white, perpendicular lines. Inside each of these small, symmetrical rectangles were two saucers of light; one was pure white and the other was a pale blue.

I lay motionless, wide awake mentally, gazing at this picture pattern for several seconds. To get a closer look, I focused my inner vision by gently crossing my eyes. Surprisingly, all the small rectangles suddenly began converging into a large one. It became so large that now all I could see on the black inner screen were the two-dimensional circles of blue and white light.

I had a funny feeling that something or someone was watching me. Maybe these two circles of light represented some sort of intelligence that knew what I was doing and thinking. On a spur-of-the-moment decision, as if believing that something could hear me, I spoke in thought, saying mentally, I want to leave my physical body.

The instant these words passed through my mind, I suddenly began lifting slowly upward. As if being pushed upward out of my physical form by some other force, I felt my arms, legs, head and chest all being slowly and methodically separated from my physical body. Gradually I started rising upward toward the ceiling, lying on my back in a horizontal position. This sudden unexpected separation caught me by surprise! My first reaction was, Wo-o-o-o-o-o, where am I going, what's happening here?

The mysterious force behind me kept pushing me slowly upward toward the ceiling. In this new weightless body I could think conscious thoughts and could feel emotions such as surprise and fear. I even had vision. I could see the bedroom ceiling high above me. I caught a brief glimpse of my brother's bed to the side of me as I floated slowly upward.

Seeing the ceiling drawing closer and closer caused me to wonder what would happen when I reached it. But lo and behold I didn't stop; the force kept pushing me slowly through the ceiling. As this happened, I could actually feel my body pass through it, as if my body was made up of a different level of energy from that of the ceiling. This whole experience was becoming more and more incredible and exciting. Here I was consciously floating through the ceiling of my brother's bedroom in a weightless, nonphysical body! Truly a sensational experience!

Now I started getting into the swing of things. Most of my fear had been replaced by joy and excitement by this time. Using my own mental thoughts I began raising myself to a vertical, standing position. When I did this, the mysterious force behind me stopped pushing and let me have full conscious control of my own movements.

I was weightlessly suspended in a dark, unfamiliar environment that appeared to be a room of some kind, presumably an attic above the bedroom. I turned to my left and saw a wall several feet away. I decided to try to pass through the wall like I'd passed through the ceiling. So I made a half-stepping, half-diving motion toward it and easily passed through it, catching my first glimpse of my body in the process.

My body's arms, hands, and legs looked the same as my physical form. And, strangely, I was wearing clothes. Dressed in blue trousers and a light colored, long-sleeve shirt, these clothes looked real. Evidently some higher power had dressed me during this experience.

After passing through the wall, I found myself somewhere outside the apartment building where my brother lived, suspended ten or fifteen feet above the ground. My thoughts went to my physical body. How was it doing without me in it? Was it still okay? The moment these thoughts entered my mind, I instantly found myself back inside my physical form again. This return was so unbelievably fast that I didn't even feel myself cross a linear distance. One moment I was somewhere outside the apartment building, and the next moment I was back in my body.

Waking abruptly, as if having just had a vivid, active dream, I reassured myself that what had happened was real. A tremendous feeling of excitement poured through me. I couldn't explain the instantaneous return to my physical body and I'd probably been out of my body not more than twenty or thirty seconds. But even so, while lying in bed thinking about what had happened, I knew this incredible experience would have a permanent and profound effect on my future.

9

A Visit To My Brother

The following morning I could still recall almost every single detail of this second out-of-body experience. Any traces of doubt still hidden in my mind as to the reality of out-of-body travel were now gone forever. An experience like this couldn't be forgotten or denied. But there were a number of things about what had happened that were confusing to me.

What were the white and blue saucers of light? What did they mean? How did they get on my inner screen? What was the strange force that had lifted me out of my physical body? In spite of these questions, this experience still made a good deal more sense to me than my first one had. Being in a visible body fit much more closely to my notion of what out-of-body travel should be like. Yet it would be some time before I understood that this was my Astral body. As Soul, I had moved into it from the physical for that experience.

As a result of this second experience, my view of death changed greatly. By stepping outside my physical body and viewing this physical world from a different perspective, the idea of death became merely a transition from life in one world to life in another world. Now the thought of dying didn't seem so ominous and terrible. It wasn't the big deal I'd always believed it to be.

Rather than saying anything to anyone about this vivid experience, I held to my oath of silence. I kept reviewing in my mind what had happened and compared my first and second experiences. There were several similarities between them. In both cases I'd left my body from the sleeping/waking state. I was fully conscious before, during, and after each experience. In both cases, while out of my body, I knew my approximate location with respect to my physical form. During both experiences the dimension of time seemed to disappear.

There were also a number of interesting differences between these two experiences. Just prior to my movement out of my body the first time, the faint high whistle in the top of my head had shifted to my right ear. This hadn't happened the second time. Reaching a high level of concentration was what had caused my first experience, but the second one had happened as a result of something lifting me out of my physical body. There had been some degree of fear about being out of my body the second time but not during the first. The second time I had a weightless body that looked and felt like my physical form. Later, I would come to know this as my Astral body. During my first experience I apparently had no body form at all. My mental capabilities had been different each time. I also remembered most of what had happened during this second adventure, but not during the first. I thought about these differences a lot during the days that followed.

About a week after this second conscious out-of-body venture, I finally decided to end my silence about what I'd experienced. My youngest brother, whom I was visiting at the time, is a very understanding person and knows me fairly well. I decided to see what his reaction would be to my second experience. Surprisingly, he listened to the tale with genuine interest. As inadequate as my explanation was, my brother's attention was obviously sincere. Upon finishing my story, I found out why when he immediately responded with a story of his own.

He told me about a television talk show he'd watched a few weeks earlier. Several people on the show talked about how they had experienced conscious out-of-body travel. According to my brother, these people didn't know how their experience had occurred, but they each insisted that it had been very real to them. One man described a critical situation in a hospital where he'd unexpectedly found himself consciously hovering above his physical body in a weightless form. It felt like his physical form and afforded him sight as well as hearing. He could see the nurse and doctor checking for vital signs. He heard the doctor pronounce him dead and became so angry that he shook his fist at the physician, wanting somehow to show him that he was still very much alive. The man decided to return to his physical body at this moment and it was then that the doctor recorded signs of life. The man's physical life was ultimately saved, enabling him to tell this story.

My brother and I talked about the subject a number of times in the following weeks. His open-mindedness to the possibility of Soul Travel was encouraging to me. It made my experience all the more real.

I stayed in the midwest for another month or so, visiting different friends and family. I continued my bedtime concentration attempts, but without success. My enthusiasm and optimism for eventually achieving another conscious out-of-body journey held strong in spite of this lack of success. My second experience was still branded vividly on my mind. I had some encouraging talks with my brother, and by this time I was also reading several more Soul Travel books written by Paul Twitchell.

The new books all emphasized the same general theme; that out-of-body travel is indeed very real but is only a first step to experiencing and proving the far greater spiritual realities of Soul and God. My primary interest in these books, however, still centered on the idea of movement out of the body.

During these weeks I tried a number of different Soul Travel methods suggested in Paul Twitchell's books as well as some concentration techniques of my own, but progress was slow. I saw little or no improvement in my ability to concentrate as the weeks passed, but I still kept trying, ever hopeful of achieving that next conscious adventure.

My brother's open-mindedness to my Soul Travel story encouraged me to talk to several of my other friends about my experience. Most of the reactions turned out positive. Two close friends told me of unusual experiences that had happened to them, and it seemed as if each individual may have consciously traveled out of his body. One of these unusual occurrences happened during sleep and the other in a relaxed, meditative state. Because neither of my friends knew anything about the possibility of Soul Travel, they both assumed that their experience had been some kind of strange, vivid dream.

Two other acquaintances who I met and talked with during those weeks had even more fascinating stories to tell.

One young lady I met was a counselor for the terminally ill. She described an experience of having drowned at the age of thirteen. She claimed that she actually felt herself pass beyond the point of death. A feeling of peacefulness and serenity came over her, and everything turned to a beautiful pink color. Later, after being revived by mouth-to-mouth resuscitation, other people she told of this experience didn't believe her story, so as time passed she viewed the experience with less and less importance.

Another fellow had an even more interesting story to tell. He told me he'd consciously been out of his body three different times. His first experience was the result of a motorcycle accident. After colliding with a car, he suddenly found himself hovering consciously above the scene of the accident in a solid, weightless body. He could see and hear everything that was going on below. He watched the lady whose car he'd hit get out of her car and run over to where his body lay. He thought he was dead, but the moment she touched him he instantly returned to his physical body.

These stories and the books that I read helped bolster my desire to Soul Travel and my willingness to try each night, despite my lack of success. I even made a rather startling and exciting find in the book *In My Soul I Am Free*. I read a description of an out-of-body experience which sounded similar to my own, where another fellow had floated upward out of his physical body through the ceiling of his bedroom.

During these weeks of unfruitful concentration my drive for that third conscious experience still stemmed mainly from the clear memory of my second encounter. All these other Soul Travel stories that I heard or read about helped reinforce my desire and belief in being able to consciously leave my body again.

10

Muffed Chance?

O ne morning, about a month and a half after my second experience, something unusual happened that rekindled my optimism. During sleep I caught a brief, conscious glimpse of a crystal-clear picture on the inner screen. This moment of consciousness caused me to wake up mentally, even though my physical body remained asleep.

Again I found myself in this spontaneous waking/ sleeping state that I had experienced before. I watched the crystal-clear picture that had formed directly in front of my inner gaze on the black screen of the mind. It consisted of a close-up pattern of the same symmetrical rectangles I'd seen just prior to my second out-of-body experience. This pattern of rectangles resembled a lit tic-tac-toe board, about three rows high and four rows wide. The rectangles were bordered with wide, yellow, perpendicular lines.

Realizing the Soul Travel potential of this situation, I quickly began trying to imagine myself in a weightless Soul body. Within seconds I had reached such a high level of concentration that it felt as if I was actually weightless. I could feel and sense myself nearing a point of separation but then, just when that critical moment came, I goofed. Mentally I held back ever so slightly, feeling just a trace of fear about leaving my body. This hint of hesitation caused the picture on my inner mind screen to suddenly vanish. Abruptly my physical body jerked awake, breaking my high level of concentration.

I felt both excited and disappointed about what had happened. Experiencing the waking/sleeping state again had been very exciting. But being held back by fear from this golden Soul Travel opportunity was disheartening. Although I felt that somehow I'd blown it, this particular incident later turned out to be very helpful to me. My sluggish Soul Travel desire got a much needed boost.

My nightly concentration attempts took on renewed vigor, but initially the results were no better than before. In order to improve my ability to concentrate, I decided to set up a daytime practice schedule. I would try picturing something in my mind as vividly as possible for a few minutes, doing this three or four times a day. Maybe my level of concentration would gradually improve, so that some of my bedtime concentration attempts would end up as out-of-body experiences.

During the coming weeks I stuck to this plan, but improvement in my ability to concentrate was minimal. About this time I started working on another riverboat. I kept up these short daily practice sessions as well as concentrating at bedtime whenever possible. My mental efforts were still just as difficult and tiring, as frustrating and time-consuming as ever. I kept trying, though, still hoping for something beneficial from this expended mental and physical energy.

Then one evening, about three weeks later, I decided to try something different. At bedtime, I would concentrate for an hour or so, strictly for practice, without caring about leaving my body. this was to be nothing more than an exercise in concentration.

I lay down in bed and tried to picture different detailed scenes in my mind. Focusing my thoughts like this was still very difficult and tiring for me. I got the idea of trying to visualize the pattern of yellow-bordered rectangles that had appeared to me several weeks earlier. As I visualized these patterns, something unexpected happened. I suddenly realized, to my total surprise and amazement, that I was no longer *imagining* what this pattern looked like; these same rectangles were now actually in front of my inner gaze on the screen of the mind.

In the instant of seeing and recognizing this crystal-clear picture on the inner screen of the mind, several thoughts flashed through me simultaneously. I immediately recognized the potential of this situation for an out-of-body journey. I also realized that my level of concentration at this precise moment was extremely high. My attention was focused one-hundred percent on the pattern of rectangles, leaving me oblivious to all other thoughts, including all thoughts of my physical body and the physical senses. And this time my physical body wasn't asleep!

I knew that the slightest break in attention would cause the picture to vanish. I remembered the mistake I'd made of mentally hesitating ever so slightly at that critical moment before. To be able to leave my body in this situation, I knew that all traces of fear and hesitation would have to be completely banished from my mind.

My desire to try to move out of the body was so strong that fear wasn't even a consideration. This time I was one-hundred percent ready and willing to let go of the physical body and flow completely with any experience that might come to me. I immediately focused my inner vision as hard as I could on this pattern of rectangles, trying to keep my mind free of all other thoughts. If I could just manage to hold this level of concentration for another couple of seconds, there might come a chance to move out of my body.

The pattern of rectangles quickly began drawing closer to my inner viewpoint. The inner screen was now taken up entirely by just one section of the yellow borderline. Focusing my inner vision as hard as possible on this still-growing section of yellow borderline, a slight suction in the vicinity of my Spiritual Eye suddenly propelled me outward into a

41

vast world of darkness. I tumbled slowly head over heels through an outer-space-like blackness. It was filled with many distant tiny white specks of light. I felt somehow energized, finer and more delicate than normal, as if mildly charged with electricity.

Fully conscious and able to feel emotions in this weightless body, I was absolutely thrilled about being out again. I loved every second of this fantastic feeling of freedom. Two months of concentration and I had finally succeeded! Thoughts of returning to my body were the furthest thing from my mind at this point; I wanted to stay out and enjoy this incredible weightless sensation as long as possible.

Within me was an inner assurance that everything would be all right. The only thing that mattered to me at this point was being happily separated from my physical body again, and having accomplished this by myself, without outside help, made me feel very proud. My previous experience had been caused by something or someone lifting me out of my physical body, but this time I'd managed to leave my body on my own.

I tumbled slowly through this seemingly endless world of darkness for perhaps three or four seconds. My surroundings suddenly changed to a lighted earthlike world. I was in what looked like a basement-type room in a house or building of some kind. I was about three feet above the floor of this room descending feet-first as if in slow motion. My first thought was that I'd moved out of the body to some place on earth. My surroundings were three-dimensional and very real; they looked just like earth.

It took a couple of seconds for me to descend to the floor of this unfamiliar, basement-like room; when my feet reached the concrete they began sinking into it. I reached out my arms, while still descending, and placed my hands solidly against the surface of the floor, stopping my descent. I pushed down on the floor solidly with my hands, bent my knees and raised my legs. Moments later I was standing up, with my feet solidly touching the floor's

42

surface. How this was possible, why I could now stand solidly on the same concrete-like floor that only moments before my feet and legs had passed through, didn't make sense to me. I hadn't a clue as to where this particular earth-like setting was or why I'd traveled to this specific place. I still felt nothing but great joy and excitement about being in this strange situation, though; the thought of fear had not even entered my mind.

I was standing in a room of average size. It was fixed up nicely with modern chairs, tables, desks, sofas, and small rugs. It looked like a family living area or rumpus room. I looked around and saw a small flight of stairs, leading to an upper-level. I started walking up the steps but quickly realized that I could mentally neutralize the pull of gravity on myself and become weightless. By imagining myself as weightless, I could mentally raise myself several feet above the steps and then use my own thought power to slowly float myself upwards through the open doorway of the next room.

The first thing I noticed in the upstairs room were two women standing about fifteen feet away from me, talking to one another. One woman was perhaps forty years old and the other maybe fifty-five. The room was decorated primarily in beige and looked like an ordinary living room in a house on earth.

I assumed that the two ladies wouldn't be able to see me, but to my surprise both women noticed me right away. They started walking slowly toward me, pointing and talking. This confused and frightened me because I thought that these two ladies weren't supposed to be able to see me. I became somewhat frightened as to what would happen if they walked over and touched me. I tried to fly away from these two approaching women, but for some reason I found myself floundering weightlessly in mid-air, able to mentally move myself forward only very slowly. The closer the two women got to me, the more nervous and afraid I became.

43

I started losing mental control about this time, probably due at least in some part to my growing apprehension. A strange sensation swept through me, and then a strong but subtle force somehow pulled me very quickly away from this lifelike environment into a world of blackness again. I knew where I was headed; back to my physical body. But in spite of the apprehension that had built up inside me during my short stay in the unfamiliar earthlike setting, I wanted to stay out of the body and enjoy this fantastic feeling of being weightless a while longer.

My desire to remain out of my body, however, didn't prevent an automatic return to it. Seconds later, without actually seeing or feeling myself reenter, I suddenly felt my physical body and physical senses surround me again and knew I was back. I immediately woke up, electrified with joy and excitement about what I'd just experienced and accomplished. I lay in bed feeling very proud of my achievement.

Thinking excitedly that maybe now the many hours of concentration effort might begin paying off, I tried to remember everything that I'd seen and heard and done during this experience. But I found that many of the details of what had happened were suddenly gone from my memory. I now couldn't consciously recall very much about the rooms of the house or the two women's faces. I couldn't even remember what they had been saying to each other. To suffer such a severe memory loss after such a neat adventure was truly a shame. After two long months of trying very hard to leave my body and finally succeeding, now only moments after returning to my body I couldn't remember very much of what had happened.

As discouraging as this sudden memory failure was, though, my soaring enthusiasm and optimism had me vibrating with excitement. I was already thinking and planning ahead for the next experience.

11

Thinking It Over

I understood that somehow I'd moved out of my physical body, presumably through the Spiritual Eye.
Having a visible body paralleled the descriptions I'd read in
my Soul Travel books, but there were many other questions
about what had happened that I couldn't answer.

The most intriguing question about this experience was
where had I projected to? Did I end up somewhere on earth,
or could I possibly have witnessed some kind of nonphysical world? The fact that the two women had been able to see
me left me wondering if maybe I'd ended up in some inner
world. According to my Soul Travel books, people on earth
aren't supposed to be able to see a person in the Soul body.

Paul Twitchell described the inner worlds as coexisting
within the same areas of space, where each inner world is
able to exist and function independently. Each is made up of
a unique level of vibration invisible to human eyes. Maybe
that meant that there existed in these inner worlds everything found in the physical world, plus anything else
imaginable.

Prior to this third projection out of my body I hadn't
given much serious consideration to the descriptions in the
reading material about inner invisible worlds. Now I had to
wonder about this possibility. Maybe the inner worlds spoken of in Mr. Twitchell's books did exist.

After waking several hours later, it was very disappointing to find that sleep had robbed my memory of even more of the details of this exciting third experience. Now I couldn't remember even half of what I'd seen and done. This undeserving memory failure didn't affect my excitement and enthusiasm, though. I was bursting to have another out-of-body experience as soon as possible. Regardless of how much sleep or mental effort would have to be sacrificed, how many days or weeks or months it would take, somehow I was going to get out of my body again, and the sooner the better. I could hardly wait for it to happen.

12

I Kick Free

A change had gradually taken place in my original
dream of someday learning how to move out of my
body to specific places on earth. Now my goal was more
simple: just getting out of the body was proving to be a
tough enough task. Where I ended up didn't matter to me
anymore. Anywhere outside my physical body would be
thrilling enough. After this third out-of-body experience,
there appeared to be a flicker of hope of achieving this goal.
That strengthened my incentive to keep trying even more.

The work schedule on the riverboat didn't allow me to do
any concentrating during my next sleep period, but I made
several short practice attempts that day. When my next
sleep period finally came, I lay down in bed and started vig-
orously trying to picture in my mind the same pattern of
yellow-bordered rectangles that I had seen the previous
evening. Concentration went poorly for me, though; my
mind wandered repeatedly to unrelated thoughts. After
maybe forty-five minutes of trying very hard to concentrate,
I began picturing other scenes in my mind. Nothing helped
me reach a high level of concentration, and eventually I fell
asleep.

During the next several days I practiced for a couple of
hours during sleep periods but saw no noticeable results. On

the fifth day something finally happened. I was again working on visualizing the pattern of brown rectangles. Being very tired mentally and needing sleep, but deciding to stick with it awhile longer, I began trying to imagine myself in a weightless body. Gradually I drifted into sleep but remained partially conscious of where I was. Half asleep, I continued to see myself as weightless and my inner legs, waist, arms, and chest began to lift out of my physical body. The inner body's head still remained intact inside my physical head, though, so I sleepily kicked my inner feet and legs up into the air as hard as I could in an all-out effort to free myself from my physical form.

The momentum of my kick tumbled me upside down and backwards out of my physical body. I fell into a vast world of darkness, my inner body finally wrenching free. The moment I separated from my physical body, my mental drowsiness disappeared and I found myself wide awake in the inner worlds. I was overjoyed about what was happening, about being out of my body again.

I did have vision in this world of darkness and could see myself moving in relation to the many distant specks of white light that dotted the surrounding blackness. Several seconds later the blackness suddenly changed to a lighted earthlike world. With crystal-clear vision I saw myself in a fully clothed inner body of the same appearance as my physical form. I was standing inside a large modern house, with furnishings just as solid and real as what's found on earth. I curiously began walking from room to room and soon discovered two guys and one gal who were about my age. Talking with them, I continued to believe that this house and these people were a part of the physical world.

After talking with these three friendly people for a short time, I was suddenly pulled away from this lifelike setting into the world of blackness again. A second or two later I ended up back inside my physical body. The disappearance of the house and the three people happened abruptly and unexpectedly, and my return through blackness was automatic, quick, and very smooth. After finding myself back inside my physical body again, I discovered to my dismay that many of the details of this exciting experience were gone from my memory.

Tremendously excited about what had happened, I had such a strong desire to move out of my body again that I began mentally trying to bring back the feeling of being in a weightless form. After focusing my thoughts like this for twenty or thirty minutes and drifting back into an early stage of sleep, I suddenly became conscious of automatically moving out of my body.

Again I found myself in a world of blackness for a few seconds and then in another solid and real earthlike world. With perfect vision and a solid, fully clothed inner body of the same appearance as my physical form, I was standing in an outdoor earthlike setting in front of a large, red brick building. With me was a short, unfamiliar, middle-aged man, sporting a black beard and dressed in a nice-looking black suit, with black top hat and a black cane. A number of other people were milling about the outdoor area. It resembled a small park with sidewalks and a large green lawn.

After talking with this fellow for what I later estimated to be ten minutes, I somehow lost control of what I was doing and quickly found myself pulled back into my physical body. This time, upon smoothly reentering my physical form, I suffered an even greater memory loss than during my previous experience. Virtually nothing remained in my memory of my lengthy conversation with the bearded stranger. Added to this disappointment was the fact that I'd now forgotten even more of my first experience.

A third time that night, once more trying my growing skill in moving out of the body, I suddenly became conscious of being out of my body in another lighted earthlike world. It was somewhat of a shock to find myself flying this time, soaring easily above an especially gorgeous coastal terrain. I flew approximately thirty feet above the ground with my arms outstretched like a glider, looking down on the ocean waves below me breaking against a rocky shoreline. I was even able to hear the waves loudly crashing against the rocks. It was unbelievably exhilarating.

Unfortunately the exhileration ended much too soon. Several minutes later I found myself being pulled away from this beautiful ocean environment into blackness again, and then into my physical body. Like my two previous reentries, this one was also accompanied by a substantial memory loss of the visual details of the experience. My feeling of excitement, joy, and pride about accomplishing these three back-to-back projections was somewhat overshadowed by my mental and physical tiredness. I rolled over and quickly fell asleep, not feeling up to doing any more concentrating this night.

13

Was It Earth or What?

The instantaneous memory loss I suffered after returning to my body from my nightly journeys was something I didn't understand and certainly didn't appreciate. Consciously leaving my physical body was so difficult and so time-consuming for me that not being able to later remember my out-of-body activities seemed nothing short of injustice.

This disappointing pattern of memory-loss didn't take anything away from my feelings of excitement about what I'd experienced during the night, though. Now my enthusiasm climbed to new heights. Three consecutive experiences in one night could only mean that I must be doing something right! Maybe my ability to concentrate was finally starting to show some improvement.

These experiences all involved worlds just as solid and real as this physical world, and being out of my body in these lifelike situations was much like being in my physical body here on earth. I had traveled in a visible inner body of the same appearance as my physical form; I could think at least some conscious thoughts and could feel emotions; I had all the body senses of touch, taste, smell, hearing, and sight, and I could solidly touch the objects around me in these worlds.

The three major differences between being in my physical body here on earth and what it was like for me to be out of the body in the lifelike situations I've described are as follows: (1) First, in these out-of-body situations, my inner self felt mildly energized compared to the way my physical body usually feels. (2) Second, the lifelike worlds I moved into obviously weren't governed by the same laws of nature as this physical world; for instance, in a couple of these out-of-body situations I did some flying. (3) Third, during some of these experiences I had only partial conscious awareness.

I was intrigued by my varying degree of awareness while out of the body. At first I hadn't realized during the earthlike experiences that I was in another world. Then during my last experience of flying over the ocean shoreline I had been consciously aware of the most minute details. There was a very noticeable difference in my conscious thinking capability during each of these latest experiences. It seemed to me that the more awake I was at the moment of departure, the more acute my out-of-body awareness became, and the better my conscious recall of the experience after I returned.

I also noticed that the way I'd reentered my physical body during these last three journeys was certainly different than before. Each of my returns had been automatic, the result of somehow being drawn away from the lifelike environment I was experiencing into a world of blackness, then moments later ending up back inside my physical body. All of these returns were so smooth that the only way I knew I'd reentered my physical form was by feeling a light jolt or detecting the presence of my physical senses surrounding me again.

By now I was becoming more and more convinced that I had actually moved into nonphysical inner worlds such as those described in my Soul Travel books. Now the descriptions in my Soul Travel books of inner planes or inner invisible worlds were becoming much more interesting to me. I was anxious to take the next step in conscious control of my journeys.

14

"I Am God!"

The following week had a very humbling effect on my optimistic plans for taking the next step in learning Soul Travel. My one- to two-hour concentration sessions nearly every sleep period netted me nothing. Imagining myself in a weightless body didn't work now any better than trying to picture the pattern of rectangles in my mind. Obviously I had still to find the sure answer to Soul Travel success.

Then about a week later I managed to leave my body again. This experience provided me with some new information about out-of-body travel. Still working on a riverboat at the time, I concentrated very hard for a couple of hours during one of my sleep periods and eventually fell asleep from sheer mental exhaustion. Then I became partially conscious of observing a dreamlike activity. My viewpoint was above the dream, and I had a sense of slowly floating forward. It seemed as if I consisted of nothing more than a bodiless pair of eyes looking down on the moving dream activity below me. I still sleepily remembered my intention to leave my body, and that half-formed thought or desire brought a sudden halt to my forward movement. Immediately I tumbled out of my physical body into the now-familiar world of blackness. I was suddenly very awake, thrilled about being out of the body again; this new kind of separation seemed to have been caused by my inner body having forward momentum.

The blackness soon changed to a lighted lifelike world, and I found myself in a situation with several other people. I don't recall exactly what happened, but I stayed with them for quite awhile, maybe thirty minutes. Then I lost mental control and returned automatically to my physical body.

Suffering such a devastating memory failure during all of these adventures seemed to me to be a pitiful shame, something I thoroughly despised and considered very unfair. The fun and thrill and freedom of being out of my body was still the greatest, even when I retained only partial recall of what had happened.

The following evening, when my sleep period finally rolled around, I drifted into an early stage of drowsiness and again became conscious of a crystal-clear picture on my inner mind screen. The picture was in full color, showing a man standing behind a narrow, wooden, dark-brown counter which resembled a small podium.

Riveting my inner vision on this crystal-clear picture caused it to quickly begin drawing closer. Within moments the scene had become so large that the man seemed lifesize. Everything in this still-picture started looking more real. Then suddenly, there was a slight suction in the vicinity of my Spiritual Eye and I found myself standing in a solid, fully clothed inner body about fifteen feet from the podium-like counter. The man in front of me was no longer two-dimensional and motionless but solid and real and alive. Somehow the two-dimensional picture which had formed on the inner screen only a few seconds before had become a very real lifelike world.

The podium stood in a wide hallway inside what appeared to be a very large building. The man behind it was maybe thirty-five years of age, of small to medium build, about five feet six inches tall with light brown hair and wearing wire-rimmed glasses. I walked up to this fellow and spoke to him briefly; he gave me a short reply and pointed toward an open doorway of a nearby room.

The room he'd pointed to was bustling with activity; people were standing around or sitting in chairs at a number of small tables situated throughout the room. There was quite a lot of noisy conversation going on. Most of the people in the room were middle-aged or older. In a far corner of the room, two women seemed to be checking in or registering the people for something that was about to happen.

I felt a little out of place here, but walked into the room anyway and sat down in an empty chair at one of the tables. There were three other people already seated at my table. I was keeping silent, just listening to the conversations going on in the room. After awhile the man sitting across from me looked at me and asked a question I'll never forget. He asked me if I was alive or dead in my physical form. Surprised, I answered that I was alive. He commented that my being so young and being able to be in this place while still alive in my physical body was quite commendable. This fellow's comment gave me the impression that the people in this room had recently died; that this place was some kind of way station. Not feeling brave enough to ask anyone about this, I never did find out.

Not long after, I was somehow drawn away from this earthlike environment into blackness and knew I was headed back to my physical body. I mentally tried to resist this automatic return by holding the weightless feeling of my inner body in my mind, mentally fighting off a return of the physical senses. A couple of seconds later my movement through blackness slowed to a near stop, giving me a sense of being very close to reentering my physical form. By continuing to hold in my mind the weightless feeling of my inner self, I felt myself slowly begin to move back through the transitional blackness again and knew that I'd succeeded in staying out awhile longer.

Moving slowly through this vast world of darkness, something unusual began to happen. I still don't understand it today and have never experienced it since, although I have read about it in my books. A deep voice began slowly speaking to me and, although the voice seemed to be coming from within me, it definitely wasn't me doing the talking. The voice began by saying, "I am God," and then continued in the same deep God-like tone for about three more sentences.

I remembered reading about this phenomenon in one of my books. I seemed to recall that a voice like this might very well speak to the beginning Soul Traveler, but that the voice wasn't really the voice of God. Therefore, in a rather brash and disrespectful manner, I interrupted the voice after it had spoken about three sentences and declared, "No, you are not God! Who are you?" I was sorry about having made this challenging and disrespectful comment, however, because the voice instantly stopped speaking.

A few seconds later the blackness suddenly vanished and I found myself surrounded by another earthlike environment. I was standing in a group of about ten other people, at what appeared to be a backyard get-together of some sort. I sat down in a lawn chair next to a couple of other fellows and just watched and listened. Very curious about where this place was, I was quite sure that the lifelike environment and these people were a part of some inner nonphysical world. I finally worked up enough nerve to ask a fellow sitting next to me where this place was. He nonchalantly replied, "The Astral Plane".

Whether it was the Astral Plane I'd projected into I couldn't say for sure then, but the Astral Plane is spoken of in Paul Twitchell's books and in other Soul Travel books as being the inner world most novice Soul Travelers begin experiencing first.

In a short while I was somehow quickly pulled away from this earthlike environment and moments later ended up back inside my physical body. Waking abruptly, rather stunned and incredibly excited about what I'd just been through, I realized that I now felt extremely well-rested and refreshed, as if having just awakened from a deep twelve hour sleep. This was surprising to me because earlier, at the moment of moving out of my body, I'd been very tired. I felt unusually happy, as if a current of love and joy was flowing through me. This feeling of love and joy stayed with me for hours afterward. Out of curiosity I checked the clock beside my bed to see how long I'd been out. Even after discounting an hour and a half for concentration, I found that I'd been separated from my physical body for approximately two hours.

15

Concentration Turns Sour

This latest experience was special enough to make me take a closer look at the information in Paul Twitchell's books. I had read about the "I am God" voice-phenomenon in one of his books; experiencing this same phenomenon soon after had to be more than just coincidence. By now I was pretty well convinced of the accuracy of his information. The more lofty spiritual concepts spoken of in his books were still hard for me to relate to, but his descriptions of the inner invisible worlds were now beginning to mean something to me.

About a week after the "I am God" experience, I got off the riverboat and again headed toward the midwest to visit friends and relatives. My next out-of-body experience occurred several days later.

Waking early one morning, I decided to try concentrating on the blackness of my inner mind screen in the vicinity of the Spiritual Eye. I gradually slipped back into sleep, and during an early stage of sleep became partially conscious of a colored picture on the inner screen. The two-dimensional still-picture showed a young lady standing in the middle of a blacktop road in an outdoor, countryside landscape. The picture grew steadily larger as I concentrated, and I felt a slight suction in the vicinity of my Spiritual Eye. Instantly

I found myself standing on the road. The young lady, with her back turned toward me, came alive and started walking away from me. It was like zooming into a stop-action movie; everything around me suddenly came to life the moment I joined that world.

My first excited impulse was immediately to do something, anything to keep my mind occupied, and hopefully stay out of the body as long as possible. My surroundings included a light blue sky and rolling, grassy hills dotted with a few shrubs and trees. The blacktop road stretched in front of me in a straight line as far as I could see. Without paying any mind to the young lady walking away from me, I jubilantly raised my inner body arms and jumped off the ground, to begin flying over this earthlike terrain. However, my exhilarating flight ended abruptly when I suddenly lost control and was pulled away into blackness, moments later ending up back inside my physical body.

I couldn't help wondering excitedly if maybe I'd finally found a good Soul Travel technique, that of focusing on the blackness of the inner screen in the vicinity of my Spiritual Eye, while allowing myself to gradually fall asleep.

Trying this same concentration method the next night and again the following morning didn't result in anything unusual, though, and my concentration sessions the next several nights and mornings fared no better. As yet no particular technique had ever proven effective for me more than once, and by this time I'd begun to figure out why. Thoughts of anticipation and apprehension would always creep into my mind while concentrating; I'd usually remember the last journey and become too excited to achieve the semi-relaxed state needed for Soul Travel. The end result in most cases was that I would concentrate for a couple of hours at bedtime and still be wide awake.

Recognizing and understanding this problem didn't help me solve it. For some reason I couldn't completely eliminate the natural emotional excitement from my thoughts when using a pattern of concentration that had previously succeeded for me. Thus each of my projections so far had been the result of experimenting with a slightly different method of concentration, when my feelings of anticipation were at a minimum and I didn't really expect success.

Therefore, several days later, I was back to experimenting with different methods of concentration again, still trying to hit on some consistent and reliable way of falling asleep and consciously leaving my body. Not for another week and a half did I manage to get out of my body, though, and this experience lasted only a few seconds.

I slowly became conscious during sleep of a dreamlike picture, a dimly lit view of a door; curiosity caused me to wonder what was on the other side. Just by thinking the thought, I suddenly passed directly through the door. On the other side I found myself weightlessly suspended in mid-air in a room that looked like a bedroom of a house here on earth. The furnishings of this room looked just as solid, real, and three-dimensional as I was used to. Only partially conscious, but thinking how neat it was to be out of the body again, and enjoying this weightlessness very much, I made the mistake of thinking about my physical body. This caused a sudden shift back into it. Disappointed about not having been able to stay out longer, but feeling very tired, I quickly fell asleep.

It was about this period of time that my desire to concentrate at nights began to sour; forcing myself to go through these long and tiring bedtime concentration sessions became increasingly difficult for me. Yet my Soul Travel enthusiasm remained as strong as ever. I was still talking enthusiastically to a few close friends and relatives about this phenomenon, and by this time I was reading several more Soul Travel books written by Paul Twitchell. But seeing so little improvement in my concentration ability over the past several months was very demoralizing. It even seemed that in recent weeks my ability to concentrate had gradually gotten a little worse. I started asking myself how could I ever hope to become an accomplished Soul Traveler

63

without first developing the ability to properly concentrate? Two hours of grueling concentration at bedtime could only go on for so long, especially when each concentration attempt gave me such poor odds of success. The fact that most of my out-of-body experiences were relatively short, and were followed by a substantial memory loss, also hurt my incentive to keep up my nightly practice.

My next experience came about a week after this latest short one. One particular evening just before bedtime, I picked up a Paul Twitchell book that I'd recently bought. It was called *The Spiritual Notebook.* I began reading about the characteristics and sounds of the different inner worlds which he claimed existed. That night I was feeling so deathly tired that after I set the book down and turned off the light, I had to mentally force myself to continue my routine of trying to imagine myself in a weightless inner body. Something must have worked despite my fatigue, because moments later I was again floating weightlessly in a world of darkness.

To my surprise, this time I started hearing the distant sound of ocean waves breaking against a shore. This sound of the waves began getting closer and louder, somehow surrounding me. Unable to see anything other than the familiar blackness dotted with distant specks of white light, I listened with sheer fascination to this captivating sound. I even remembered having read in *The Spiritual Notebook* only a few hours earlier about the sound of the Astral Plane being "the roar of the sea." I listened to this rhythmic ocean-wave melody for maybe ten seconds, and then was quickly drawn back into my physical body bringing an abrupt halt to this sound. Feeling very tired at this point but curious about what had happened to me, I again mentally forced myself to concentrate and the same thing happened as before. I again heard the sound of ocean waves crashing loudly against a shore and then was pulled back into my physical body.

About two weeks after hearing the sound of ocean waves on the inner planes I moved to another riverboat. During the month spent working there, I got out of the body only once. The work schedule was difficult, but mainly my desire to sacrifice time, sleep, and mental energy for concentration just wasn't very strong.

I did have one experience during that month. I became partially conscious during sleep and had a vivid, active dream in which I realized consciously that the dream world I was viewing wasn't a dream at all; I was surrounded by a very real, three-dimensional, earthlike world. In my inner body, I was taking an active part in this dreamlike sequence of events which involved several other people. After returning to my body a short while later, I went back to sleep, concentrating in some manner and during sleep moved out of the body once more that night with some degree of consciousness.

16

Enthusiasm for Soul Travel Sags

By the time I got off the riverboat after working for a month, my desire to concentrate at nights had all but fizzled out. My snail-paced Soul Travel progress had come to a halt. The strain and difficulty of continuous forced concentration had gotten to be too much even for me. On the occasional night when I tried to coax myself into concentrating at bedtime, my mind simply began refusing to obey. This may sound strange, but my mind actually began refusing to go through any more long concentration sessions, regardless of my determination or will power. Accepting this fact was tough for me because it apparently meant the end of my Soul Travel career. I didn't know of any other way to leave my body at that point, except by means of concentration.

Also, without any new or recent out-of-body adventures to think about, my sagging Soul Travel enthusiasm had to come from my memory of past experiences. The passing of time gave a storybook quality to each of my past successes. The more distant they became, even my more vivid and thrilling ones, the less I remembered about them and the less real and important they seemed to me.

17

Six Months after My First
Out-of-Body Experience

Finally things shifted. There came another major turning point in my Soul Travel story. Here's how it
happened.

Several weeks after getting off the riverboat, I drove to
the midwest again. One evening before undertaking something very important the next day, I felt somewhat nervous
at bedtime and woke in the middle of the night after just a
couple hours sleep. Lying in bed resting and relaxing, trying to doze off again but unable to fall asleep because of
thinking about what was to happen the next day, I could
hear the faint high whistle in the top of my head. In a totally
relaxed way I gazed steadily at the blackness of the inner
screen. My thoughts didn't include Soul Travel; they
revolved around the important event of the coming day and
getting as much rest as possible before morning.

I lay quietly in bed for a couple of hours, trying to fall
asleep again. Then something totally unexpected happened.
A fuzzy picture began to form in the blackness in front of
my inner vision. It seemed odd in my wide-awake condition. This hadn't happened before. The picture kept getting
larger and clearer and within perhaps three or four seconds
had become so large that it filled my entire inner screen.

Now only slightly blurred, this earthlike scene showed a couple of houses, a lawn, a sidewalk, and a street.

I was still very surprised that my being wide-awake hadn't yet caused this picture to disappear. I quickly and carefully focused my inner gaze and my full attention on the scene, trying to rid my mind of all thoughts of my physical body and the physical world. Immediately the picture began drawing closer and then began surrounding my inner point of vision. Something about this earth scene began looking familiar to me, and then suddenly it struck me—I knew where this place was! It looked like a place on earth near my hometown in Iowa.

Recognizing this place stirred tremendous excitement in me. I felt a slight suction in the vicinity of my Spiritual Eye and instantly moved into the picture. My first excited impulse after traveling into the scene was to run to the house where I used to live. Literally vibrating with joy and excitement about being out of my body again, I ran down a nearby familiar-looking alley. As I ran I noticed that the scenery seemed slightly new to me. The house and backyard that should have been my previous home looked a bit different, so I drew the conclusion that I was in some inner world.

While still running at full-speed down the alley, I made a two-legged jump, springing off the ground like off of a diving board, and I soared up into the light blue sky. I used my thought power to level myself off at about fifty feet above the ground and flew through the air with my arms outstretched like glider wings. It was absolutely incredible!

After flying just a short ways, I passed over a white house where a middle-aged man was sitting outside on the porch. It was obvious from the way this fellow looked up at me that he could see me. Being visible to this man gave me my second clue that the world beneath me was likely some inner world and not earth.

It wasn't long before I reached the outskirts of the city and the landscape below me changed drastically. Flying now in a direction away from the city, I saw the terrain beneath me change to a gorgeous rocky landscape resembling many small, connected cliffs; the most striking thing about this unusual rock terrain was the beautiful color combinations. These cliffs below me ranged in color from soft beige to deep, rusty brown, making this a landscape far more spectacular than any landscape I had seen on earth.

Mentally guiding myself down, I gently landed feetfirst in the midst of the rock formations. I just stood there for awhile, passively marveling at the scenery, somewhat awed by the beauty of it. My mind ran out of thoughts at this point, though, which was a mistake. Seconds later I felt the first telltale signs of losing control. Not wanting to return automatically to my physical body, I quickly began trying to refill my mind with thoughts, hurriedly trying to imagine something that would keep me there. Despite my desire and mental efforts an increasingly powerful force from above began pulling at me. Just as my feet lifted off the ground, I remembered the important event that was to happen to me the next day. For some reason I hurriedly shouted outloud, "God, I am a part of You," hoping that something or someone might hear me and be impressed with this spiritual remark, maybe helping to turn the outcome of the coming day's event in my favor. Moments later I was pulled upward into blackness and back into my physical body.

I returned and abruptly jerked awake, ecstatic about what had happened. My wounded Soul Travel enthusiasm was instantly healed. After having all but given up on experiencing any more conscious journeys out of my body, this unexpected experience was like a bonus to me, a second chance at Soul Travel. With this feeling fresh in my mind again, I now wanted more. I was back on the Soul Travel path again.

18

A New Clue to Soul Travel

The reason this latest Soul Travel experience was so very important to me was the way I had left my body—in a state of total relaxation. All my previous experiences had been the result of a long, tiring, and grueling concentration session which was why I'd finally given up on concentration as an out-of-body technique. Now, with proof of being able to leave my body in a totally relaxed state, my desire to learn more and to do more experimenting was reignited.

Piecing together the answer to a relaxed, easy way of leaving my body wouldn't happen right away and would surely require some effort and sacrifice. I knew this, but knowing that the answer I was searching for did exist made all the difference in my renewed enthusiasm.

For the next several weeks I tried almost every night to duplicate the sequence of events that had preceded this latest inspiring trip out of my body, hoping to solve the puzzle of the relaxed way of Soul Travel. Driving westward now, intending to spend several months touring the northwest United States and parts of Canada, I was not being burdened by any daily schedules or timetables and had plenty of free time to experiment at nights with different relaxed ways of listening to the faint high whistle and gazing at my inner screen. But about the only thing I learned those weeks from these relaxed, trial-and-error attempts to leave my body was that gazing passively at the black inner screen for any length of time wasn't so easy. During these attempts my mind would start jumping from one thought to another, the result being that most of the practice sessions resulted in my simply falling asleep.

As the weeks passed without any further rewards for my Soul Travel efforts, my enthusiasm and optimism about out-of-body travel began to slide again, and gradually my relaxed bedtime Soul Travel attempts became fewer and fewer.

Six weeks later, I was driving through a western province of Canada and stopped at a rest area for awhile. Feeling tired I lay down in a comfortable position and closed my eyes. I made a special point not to allow myself to fall asleep because of wanting to drive a ways further that afternoon. With no thoughts whatsoever about Soul Travel, I began gazing at the blackness of the inner screen and listening to the faint high whistle in my head.

Suddenly I became conscious of a colored picture on my inner screen, directly in front of my vision. I immediately focused my inner gaze and my full attention on this crystal-clear scene. As had happened before, the picture quickly began drawing closer. But just when my attention on this now-close-up, three-dimensional picture became perfect and that opportune moment for moving out of my body presented itself, mentally I held back ever so slightly, feeling just a trace of fear. It had all happened so fast and been so unexpected. I wasn't one-hundred percent ready and willing to let go of my physical body at that crucial moment. Suddenly the picture vanished, and I abruptly jerked awake, another perfect Soul Travel opportunity gone.

Sorry about having blown this surprise opportunity to leave my body, I was still glad to have experienced it. What had happened had given me some new clues to figuring out

74

a relaxed way of leaving my body. This time I had maintained a constant vague awareness of who and where I was while surrendering myself to a state of total relaxation, near to falling asleep. Excited about the potential of this new tidbit of information, I looked forward to bedtime that evening, curious about whether this picture-phenomenon might happen again when trying the same method of relaxation.

19

What About Relaxation?

T hat evening when bedtime came, I anxiously lay
down and started relaxing in the same manner as I'd
done that afternoon, but nothing out of the ordinary happened. After a time I drifted into sleep. The next evening
was the same story, but I persistently tried again at bedtime
the evening after. I relaxed, gazed at the black inner screen,
and listened to the faint high whistle in the top of my head,
while also maintaining a constant vague awareness of who
and where I was. Again nothing unusual happened, and
eventually I drifted into sleep. But when I awoke unexpectedly in the middle of the night, my desire to try to move out
of the body was still fairly strong. I decided to give this
relaxation procedure another try.

This time something happened. Feeling tired and sleepy,
I began gazing at the blackness of the inner screen and listening to the faint high whistle in my head. To keep from
mentally falling asleep, I held that constant relaxed awareness of my own identity. Resting like this for maybe forty-
five minutes or an hour, I suddenly became conscious of a
colored picture on my inner mind screen.

My reaction to seeing this was by now automatic. As I
focused my inner gaze and my full attention on this picture,
it began drawing closer to my inner point of vision.

Remembering my earlier mistake of holding back at that critical moment, I began mentally reassuring myself in thought, saying things like, Stay calm, stay relaxed, don't be afraid. By the time the picture had surrounded my inner vision, I had swept all traces of fear from my mind, and when that critical moment of leaving the body presented itself, I was one-hundred percent ready to go.

Moving instantly into an earthlike scene, I found myself in a three-dimensional room; several other unfamiliar young men and women were also present in this room taking part in some kind of activity. I immediately joined them, wanting to stay busy to keep my mind occupied and to hopefully reduce the chances of an automatic return to my physical form. Apparently a good portion of my thoughts and actions during this experience were influenced by my subconscious mind; some of my reactions seemed rather automatic. Today only a few meaningless fragments of information still remain in my notes as to what sort of group activity I got involved in during this experience. Awhile later I was pulled into blackness, but by mentally trying very hard to hold onto the weightless feeling of my inner body, I managed to remain suspended out-of-body. A short time later, I ended up in another inner lifelike world.

My notes are brief on this second experience, as well, so I can't describe from memory what happened. Later, after returning to my body, I succeeded in moving out once more, using this same method of relaxation. The picture-phenomenon happened again, enabling me to move out once more. Here again, though, my notes describe more about how I got out of my body rather than what happened during the experience.

I went back to sleep after this, feeling very proud about what I'd accomplished. My conscious awareness during these experiences hadn't been all that good, and my recall of what I'd seen and done while I was out was basically poor. But to have twice witnessed the picture-phenomenon using the same relaxation procedure as that of several days earlier was very encouraging and exciting. Just how much Soul Travel potential this relaxation technique would show me in the future remained to be seen. Already my hopes were high. Maybe I had finally found an easy way of leaving my body.

I couldn't stop thinking all that next day about my discovery. When evening came, I eagerly went to bed early and began practicing my new technique. Nothing happened, though, and eventually I drifted into sleep. Again I awoke unexpectedly in the middle of the night and decided to make another try at relaxation. Maybe forty-five minutes later, after slipping into a near-sleep state, the picture-phenomenon happened again. By quickly focusing my inner vision very hard on this crystal-clear picture, I moved into the scene. My memory of this experience is poor, probably because my out-of-body conscious awareness was only mediocre, but it was especially thrilling to have been successful using this same method of relaxation twice.

The next night my new Soul Travel method failed me, however, both at bedtime and again after waking in the middle of the night. Having successfully moved out of the body the past two nights caused me to feel a little apprehensive about being able to leave my body again. This kept me from fully relaxing during both the next night's attempts. By consciously waiting for the picture-phenomenon to materialize again, I unknowingly prevented myself from relaxing and drifting into the essential near-sleep state.

The next night I tried the new method once again but eventually fell asleep with nothing unusual happening. Early that morning I awoke unexpectedly and decided to make one more Soul Travel attempt. This time it finally worked!

Becoming conscious of a colored picture on the black inner screen, I immediately focused my inner vision and moved into the picture. I only stayed in this lifelike situation perhaps a few minutes, however, before losing control and returning automatically to my body.

Three successful Soul Travel nights out of four was a fantastic percentage for me, and at this point my feelings of pride and enthusiasm about my newfound relaxation procedure were very strong. I even felt somewhat confident about being able to leave my body again the next night, provided of course I had the desire to try and the willingness to sacrifice some time and sleep.

It's almost humorous for me to look back and think of the cockiness that had grown inside me after this third successful Soul Travel night. Although not showing outwardly yet, deep within me were budding feelings of being different or better than other people because of what I'd discovered. I chuckle now at this case of growing overconfidence. How short a period of time this feeling lasted!

Surprise, surprise, just when my Soul Travel hopes were starting to build, when I thought the hard part was finally behind me, that I'd finally figured out how to leave my body, the effectiveness of my new Soul Travel technique disappeared just as quickly as I'd discovered it. I had no luck whatsoever during the following weeks trying to duplicate the pattern of the previous journeys.

I knew exactly what was going wrong, too. My emotions of anticipation and apprehension were the cause of this sudden and extended lack of success. As my confidence began to grow, my nighttime relaxation sessions became less relaxed. I wasn't able to achieve the delicate balance of staying alert yet allowing myself to drift into a near-sleep state.

I grudgingly began to accept the fact that too many variables had to fit and flow just perfectly in order for the picture-phenomenon to occur. I decided that my only alternative to eventual Soul Travel success was to start experimenting again with other relaxation techniques, preferably techniques similar to this latest one. Maybe by doing some more experimenting, I could find some other relaxed Soul Travel method that would prove to be more consistent and reliable than my latest flash-in-the-pan.

20

Enter Contemplation

I began reading again in Paul Twitchell's books and was struck by his statements about something called contemplation. He spoke of it as a far better approach to Soul Travel than either meditation or concentration. This began to mean something to me. Unknowingly I'd been using contemplation in this latest Soul Travel method of relaxation. It gradually dawned on me that I'd made a transition in the past months from concentration to contemplation.

Because it is so very important for all aspiring Soul Travelers to understand how valuable a tool contemplation can be, I'm going to spend a short chapter here describing in my own words the difference between meditation, concentration, and contemplation.

The word *meditation* seems to cover a wide variety of different mental practices. My definition of meditation goes something like this: Meditation involves trying to achieve a completely relaxed, totally passive state of body and mind. Ideally this is accomplished by first relaxing the physical body as much as possible and then throwing the mind blank, trying to free the mind of all thoughts concerning the physical body and the physical world. Meditation can be practiced for any number of reasons, including reducing daily mental stress and tension.

I can say nothing bad about meditation. Many people scoff at such a practice, but most of these people haven't tried it. For the relatively calm person or for the individual carrying a great deal of mental stress, a daily meditation routine will almost surely result in a surprising reduction of internal tension within just a matter of days or weeks.

Concentration is just the opposite of meditation. The only good thing I have to say about concentration is that it enabled me to achieve my first few conscious trips out of the body. I'll be forever grateful to concentration for giving me proof of the reality of out-of-body travel, but under no circumstances would I ever go back to concentration as a means of Soul Traveling. I would also never advocate this form of mental torture to anyone else.

My definition of concentration, based on my own futile learning attempts, is this: Concentration is an attempt to rigidly force the mind to hold a specific idea or visual picture, trying to lock the mind so perfectly onto this single idea or picture that all attention is withdrawn from the physical body and physical surroundings. Reaching a perfect level of concentration is extremely difficult, but if achieved, even just for a moment, separating from the physical body then becomes quite easy.

Contemplation is more of a happy medium between meditation and concentration, not passive like meditation and yet not nearly as mentally and physically draining as concentration. Based on my own learning efforts these past few years, my definition of contemplation goes like this: Contemplation is a relaxed pointing of the mind in one certain direction, a continuous dwelling on some feeling, thought, or idea in as relaxed a manner as possible. In contemplation one does not try to rigidly affix the mind to anything but instead allows it to wander and simply brings it back each time it strays off.

Contrary to the way it may sound, contemplation isn't always easy. However, for purposes of moving out of the body, contemplation offers two important advantages:

simplicity and effectiveness. It doesn't take months or years to learn how to contemplate, and there aren't any great tricks or natural abilities required. Anybody can contemplate. Even the person who's never experienced conscious out-of-body travel can do so using this technique. The only requirement for the beginning Soul Traveler is that the contemplation effort must be genuine, wholehearted, and determined.

21

I Hear of the Godman

Although my progress at learning to contemplate was not fast, I did manage two out-of-body projections during the next several weeks. Both were very short but still exciting, important, and helpful to me in keeping my Soul Travel enthusiasm alive.

The first of these two experiences happened using the same relaxation procedure as I'd tried several weeks earlier. After contemplating at bedtime and eventually falling asleep, I awoke unexpectedly in the middle of the night and, by imagining myself in a weightless inner body, moved automatically into a world of blackness. Only a few seconds later I was drawn back into my physical body, however, and soon fell asleep.

About a week later I lay down one afternoon for a short nap and without even contemplating became conscious during sleep of observing the black inner screen. Moments later a picture appeared and by quickly focusing my inner gaze on this picture, I succeeded in moving out of the body. I ended up in a world of blackness instead of in the picture and returned to my body only a few seconds later. I went back to sleep imagining myself again in a weightless body, and during an early stage of sleep became conscious once more of moving out of my body into blackness. Of interest, at the moment of leaving my body this second time, something snapped in the area of my Spritual Eye which momentarily felt a little painful. This snap was so loud that it sounded like one of my eyelids had popped open and shut. About this time a truck drove past my motor home, causing a quick, automatic return to my physical form.

Whenever I'm out of the body, any noise or movement around me will cause a quick, automatic return to my physical form. Somehow I can hear or detect these noises or movements through the physical body's senses. I wondered at the time how I could be consciously separated from my physical form yet still be somehow linked to it.

In several of his books Paul Twitchell speaks of a silver cord, saying that each person is endowed with a stretchable, umbilical-like cord which connects the physical body to several of the inner bodies and is severed only at physical death. It could be because of this silver cord that I can be out of body in an inner body and still be able to hear or detect noises or movements around my physical body through the physical senses. What little I know about this silver cord comes from my Soul Travel books, but I'm quite certain it does exist.

One night not too many months ago I managed to sleepily crawl out of my physical body after becoming partially conscious during sleep. While standing next to my bed in an inner body I saw a silver cord, maybe a quarter-inch in diameter, dangling down from the back of my head across my chest, coiling around my feet onto the floor. It felt something like flexible plastic tubing and seemed to be rather delicate. A gentle tug on it caused a mild pain at the spot where it was attached to my head. The lack of light didn't allow me to see much and only a few seconds later I lost control and returned to my body automatically. I've never felt or been aware of a cord attached to my head during any other of my out-of-body experiences.

Soon it was time to start heading back to the midwest to go to work on another riverboat. I resumed my nighttime contemplations during the week spent slowly driving back to the midwest. Incredibly, I managed to leave my body five nights out of seven, an amazing success average for me. These nightly contemplations of mine weren't easy; all of them seemed to last a couple of hours or more, and I had to experiment with several different patterns of contemplation to achieve any conscious experiences. But by the end of this outstanding week I was in the clouds, hardly able to believe my Soul Travel success. The prospects of me becoming a more proficient Soul Traveler were looking so encouraging that my whole personality began radiating the joy and excitement I felt inside.

Here's how my five successful Soul Travel nights unfolded.

The first night I contemplated lightly at bedtime for about thirty minutes, gazing at the black inner screen and listening to the faint high whistle in my head. I kept repeating to myself that I wanted to move out of my body that night. Then I just went to sleep. I woke up in the middle of the night and contemplated diligently, but nothing out of the ordinary happened and I ended up falling asleep again. When I woke up unexpectedly several hours later, I decided to try contemplating once more. I gradually drifted into a light sleep and suddenly became conscious of automatically moving out of my body into blackness, then seconds later ending up in a lighted lifelike world. The only part of this experience that I later remembered was flying over an extremely beautiful landscape very unlike earth.

The next night I had a similar experience using the same method of contemplation, leaving my body in much the same way, and finding myself surrounded by a lifelike world. During this experience I was with a person who looked and talked like one of my brothers. Later I puzzled over how one of my family members could have been with me in this out-of-body situation. Did something or someone impersonate my brother for some reason, or was it possible to be with a family member in out-of-body circumstances?

Could this person have even been my brother in one of his inner bodies?

The following night I again moved out of my body in much the same way, making this three successful nights of traveling in a row, a very exciting first for me. At first I didn't really think I was going to be able to leave my body because my feelings of anticipation and apprehension were having a disruptive effect on the contemplation session. I finally fell asleep with nothing unusual happening, but after waking unexpectedly several hours later, I automatically moved out of my body. This session started out to be rather unique and fun; without even trying I did a perfect slow-motion back flip out of my physical body.

After passing through blackness for a few seconds, I found myself inside a room with maybe ten other people. I recall making an enthusiastic speech to this group of people, waving my arms around and using a lot of hand gestures. I also discovered an interesting phenomenon; while doing some flying later in the experience, I succeeded in twice passing through the solid wall of a building. It took thinking very hard about wanting to do it, but somehow I was able to change the vibration level of my inner body enough to allow me to slowly extend it through the wall. The difference between the energy and vibration of my inner body as compared to that of the wall was very noticeable, and it took good concentration to accomplish this feat.

During my next inner experience, I met and fell head over heels in love with a young lady on one of the inner planes. Later I was to recognize this as the Astral Plane. As yet I haven't truly fallen in love with any female here on earth in this physical life so this experience was very surprising to me. I was with this young woman for quite awhile, perhaps thirty or forty-five minutes, and still felt a great deal of love for her hours after finally being drawn back into my physical form.

Several nights later I found myself flying again, this time over an unearthly terrain of exceptional beauty; the surface of the ground below me was seemingly made up of color combinations of light. I tried to remember this gorgeous scenery after returning to my body but unfortunately I could only recall a small portion of it.

I had one more experience that same night. It began my search for the Godman. I was in a house, walking around and asking several people nearby if they knew anything about the Spiritual Master spoken of in Paul Twitchell's books.

This was an important turning point for me and something I'm going to explain. One of the fundamental spiritual ideas put forth in nearly all of Paul Twitchell's books is that there has always been and will always be a living Godman here on earth. When this Godman moves on from the physical realm to other duties in the inner worlds, another spiritually-advanced person on earth has already been chosen and trained by him to become the next focal point or channel for Spirit into the physical worlds and all the inner worlds as well.

This flow of Spirit moves through the Godman's body with such intensity that touching him can sometimes result in a mild electric shock. Each Godman assumes the same duty; to serve as a channel for the message of God in all the physical and nonphysical worlds, and to use the powers and abilities that come with being a channel for Spirit to give spiritual assistance and guidance to all who ask for it. In his "radiant Inner body" the Godman's capabilities are unlimited. Being one and the same with Spirit in his "radiant form," the Godman is capable of miracles, can manifest more than one visible body anywhere in the physical or inner worlds; and in Spirit form can be in all places at all times and know all things.

He helps each chela (student, follower, disciple) gradually unfold spiritually, using dreams as his primary means of teaching and giving assistance, but helping in a host of other ways, too. He can help heal and dissolve a chela's past and present karma, and travel with a chela on conscious journeys into the inner worlds. Although the two faces of the Godman, his physical self and his inner self, are always linked together, the Inner Master is by far the most versatile and most important part of the Godman.

Naturally a written description about such an amazing individual isn't one that most people can readily accept without seeing some sort of proof, myself included. But by this time I was becoming more and more curious about the spiritual adepts that Mr. Twitchell kept referring to in his books. To begin with, I couldn't imagine how one person could be in all places at all times, but with all that I'd experienced thus far I couldn't automatically rule this possibility out. After all, a year earlier I wouldn't have dreamed it possible for anyone to be able to even leave the physical body!

Getting back to my most recent out-of-body experience, I was hoping to locate this so-called Godman and thought he ought to be somewhere around this inner plane I was visiting. But none of the people I asked knew anything about him. I even tried calling his name outloud, thinking that maybe he might somehow be able to hear me, but there was no response. I never did find him that night.

Lying in bed the next morning, I thought about what had happened during the night and an interesting idea came to me. In a way, I seemed to be living two different lives. When I was actually out of my physical body, I was very conscious of exactly what I was doing in the other worlds but oftentimes didn't remember much about my physical life. The opposite was true of my waking hours here on earth: while consciously awake in my physical body, I knew all about my physical life but very little about my inner activities.

This three-and-a-half month trip to the northwest turned out to be invaluable to me and my future in Soul Travel. It somehow kept my Soul Travel career from sputtering and dying out. I had had a lot of free time, was able to sleep late in the mornings, and could contemplate for rather long periods of time at nights. This was a big help to me. Most of my contemplation sessions lasted an hour and a half to two hours. It wasn't uncommon for me to need a couple of extra hours of sleep in the morning.

This latest series of five successful Soul Travel nights out of seven gave flashing signs that the answer I was searching for might be just around the corner. Filled with a wealth of new information about how to proceed, my confidence had reached new heights. One especially useful bit of information that I had picked up during these months was that my odds were better in the middle of the night rather than at bedtime. At that time it seemed more of a certainty for me to be able to drift into a light sleep while contemplating, which improved my chances of success.

22

My Experiments Pay Off

A needy financial condition prodded me to spend most of the next three months working on riverboats, and my Soul Travel progress slowed considerably during this time. I still managed about ten conscious trips out of the body during these three months, though, which I considered a pretty good achievement.

Before highlighting the more interesting of these experiences, I should first mention that no particular pattern of contemplation proved consistently effective for me during these months. I tried using all sorts of different contemplative techniques I was so far familiar with: (1) imagining myself in a weightless body inside my physical body, (2) imagining myself in a weightless body outside my physical body, (3) imagining myself in a circular-shaped weightless form, (4) listening to the faint high whistle in the top of my head, (5) observing the black inner screen in different ways, (6) trying to observe one small white speck of light on the black inner screen, (7) keeping a constant vague awareness of my own identity while going to sleep, (8) letting go of all mental ties with the physical body and physical world and trying to shift my inner point of awareness further and further away from my physical head into blackness, and others. But only occasionally did one of these trial-and-error contemplation attempts result in a conscious out-of-body journey for me.

My old familiar enemies, anticipation and apprehension, were the main reason for my lack of consistent out-of-body success. Every time a technique worked successfully, these two nagging emotions would crowd into my thoughts and make it much more difficult for me to relax. My sacrifice of time and sleep and mental effort still proved to be a very worthwhile investment for me, though.

One afternoon several days after getting on the riverboat, I lay down in bed, went to sleep without contemplating, and became partially conscious during sleep of a strange, weightless, wave-like feeling coming over me. Realizing that something was happening, I remained unafraid and consciously surrendered myself completely to this wavy, floating sensation. Moments later I moved out of the body into a lifelike world, returning only a few seconds later. Twice during the next three months on the riverboat this happened to me; becoming conscious during sleep of automatically moving out of my body without having contemplated beforehand.

A couple of weeks later after contemplating at bedtime and falling asleep, I became vaguely conscious of a vivid, active dream in progress. I slowly became conscious of the fact that this wasn't a dream at all; surprisingly I was already separated from my physical form, moving in an inner body in the midst of a solid inner world. I was able to assume conscious control of most of my thoughts and actions during the remainder of this experience.

The very next day, after contemplating at bedtime by imagining myself in an oval-shaped weightless form, I drifted into sleep and became conscious of moving out of my body into blackness. I tumbled slowly through this world and was suddenly aware of a partially transparent, bluish face of a man appearing beside me in the darkness. It disappeared several seconds later when I descended into a lifelike world.

After returning to my body maybe five minutes later, I drifted back to sleep and the same thing happened again. During an early stage of sleep I became conscious of moving out of my body, and the same bluish, two-dimensional face of a man appeared beside me as I tumbled slowly through darkness in a weightless inner body. After I returned I wondered about this, remembering that several of Paul Twitchell's books described how the face of the Inner Master can sometimes appear to the Soul Traveler in this way. From what my memory still held of these two experiences, though, the face I'd seen didn't match the picture of the present-day Master shown in several of my Paul Twitchell books.

Several days later an even more unusual experience happened. After contemplating at bedtime, holding a vague awareness of my own identity while also thinking of my inner point of awareness moving further and further away from my physical head into blackness, eventually I drifted into sleep and suddenly became conscious of standing in an earthlike world. The sky above me was dimly lit, almost black, and the flat landscape around me stretched in all directions as far as the dim light allowed me to see. Curiosity about this place prompted me to lift my arms, jump off the ground, and begin flying over this terrain. There were no signs of people or buildings or trees anywhere. I felt rather lost and alone flying over this rather drab, barren landscape and decided to try to mentally change this environment if I could. Landing gently on the ground feetfirst, I closed my eyes and started concentrating very hard on trying to change my surroundings.

Without warning a tremendous surge of energy instantly penetrated my inner body and the whole area around me; it immediately put me to my knees. My face contorted from the somewhat painful effect of the intense energy, and suddenly I saw in front of me the open doorway to a room of some kind. The previous drab earthlike landscape had suddenly changed to another environment. Unable to withstand more than a few seconds of this penetrating energy, I quickly lost control and shifted back inside my physical body.

There seemed only one logical explanation for this phenomenon I had experienced. I must have inadvertently shed one of my inner bodies and taken on another of a greater vibration, shifting to a higher inner plane. According to my Soul Travel books this was possible, for Soul works with several different inner bodies which vibrate at differing rates of energy.

A couple of weeks later another very interesting and very important experience occurred. On this particular evening I went to sleep listening to a cassette tape concerning the subject of Eckankar and Soul Travel. During sleep I became partially conscious of an unusually vivid dream in progress.

The dream began with a man talking to me. He was dressed in a long, flowing white robe, his robe seemingly made up of white light, and throughout this dream I consisted of nothing more than a bodiless point of view. I listened to this man but consciously heard no sounds or voices during the dream and therefore couldn't tell what was being said.

After awhile the man stopped talking, got up, and walked a short distance through the blackness to where another man was sitting. The second man began talking with me and the subject of Soul Travel came up; I guess I mentally asked him something about how to move out of my body. The first man raised his right arm and pointed two fingers at my Spiritual Eye. Consciously focusing my dream viewpoint on his pointed fingers, I suddenly moved out of my body.

I moved swiftly through a vast world of darkness and this caused me to feel somewhat lost and disoriented. A bit worried about my destination, I decided to return to my physical body of my own accord. Imagining my physical senses coming back, I quickly found myself back inside my physical body again, but sadly could no longer remember what the two men's faces had looked like.

Two weeks later another one of my unusual out-of-body experiences occurred. One night I suddenly became conscious of a strange floating sensation while lightly sleeping, and by surrendering myself completely to this feeling, moments later I was jerked upward a foot or two above my physical body into a world of blackness. I lay on my back and felt a force behind me begin lifting me upward into a vertical standing position. I was pushed slowly forward though the surrounding darkness, motionless and unafraid, surrendering myself completely to the force behind me. I felt certain that no harm would come to me, and soon found myself in a lighted earthlike world, standing now in front of the doorway of a large, white building.

Thrilled about being out of my body again, my immediate reaction was to joyfully run though the open doorway in front of me. I was running down a long, narrow hallway of this large, white building when I clearly heard a loud noise just outside the room, back where my physical body lay. Thinking that someone was about to walk into the bedroom where my body was, and being terrified at the thought that someone might see my physical body without me in it, I tried desperately to return. But at that instant I couldn't do so. Not until several seconds later, after somehow being whisked away from this lifelike inner world, and then pushed though blackness at a high rate of speed by some other force, did I reenter my physical form and jerk my body awake. As it turned out, my fears of someone opening the door of my bedroom were unfounded; the loud noise had been caused by a large object falling to the floor in the next room.

Several days later another memorable experience happened. I suddenly became conscious of being out of my body watching several people endure a strange Hell-like situation. Being rather frightened by the sight in front of me, I remember thinking to myself that I was going to get my act together so as not to have to go through anything like this after death. Wanting to leave this awful place as quickly as possible, I raised my arms, jumped off the ground, and began flying in the opposite direction through a dark sky.

A large city became visible on the ground below me, lighted by a number of floodlights from high up in the black sky. Flying toward this city area, I landed feetfirst near a large, modern building which I definitely recognized. Consciously I didn't know what this building was for or where this place was, but without a doubt I'd seen this building before and it seemed I'd seen it recently.

A large, circular-shaped astrological design in the wide walkway leading up to the two large front doors was also familiar to me. Trembling with excitement about recognizing this building, I walked up to the two large front doors, but then on the spur-of-the-moment I decided not to go inside; I was somehow afraid that seeing the inside of the building might overexcite me and cause an automatic return to my physical body. Wanting to stay out of my body as long as possible and near to being too excited anyway, I turned and hurriedly walked away. Shortly thereafter I flew to another part of this city and became involved in another activity which I didn't record.

Three weeks later I had my finest and most unexplainable series of experiences to date. After contemplating and drifting into sleep, I suddenly became conscious of being out of the body inside a room of some large, older building. With me were two young ladies about my age. Interestingly enough, one of them was familiar to me; I even knew her name. She knew and recognized me, too, but it wasn't from my present physical life. Evidently she and I had met in some past life or in some previous inner-world situation. With good conscious awareness of what was happening, I talked with this gal for awhile, and then both women began explaining to me something about the make-up of the physical body. The room we were in resembled an outdated medical laboratory.

After returning from this experience, I remained motionless and went back to sleep trying a new and different way of contemplation. I remembered Paul Twitchell's claims about the existence of a true living Godman here on earth, so I began slowly and softly repeating this man's name over and over, trying to drift into sleep this way. It took me ten or fifteen minutes to drift back into a light sleep, chanting softly like this. Then suddenly I became conscious of automatically shifting outside my physical body into a world of blackness — with no detectable body form at all. I may have had some kind of circular or oval weightless shape in this situation, but as far as I could tell I consisted of nothing more than a bodiless point of vision with full conscious awareness. In front of me was a rectangular picture in full color.

Strangely enough, this picture couldn't be observed directly; looking straight at it would cause it to disappear and then reappear to the right of my vision. To keep it from repeatedly disappearing and reappearing, I had to view it from a slight angle. The picture showed a crystal-clear color scene of a man sitting in a chair. I immediately recognized the man in the picture as being the Living ECK Master, whose name I'd been chanting earlier, before drifting into sleep. His appearance matched the pictures of him in my Soul Travel books.

This was a live, moving scene rather than a still-picture. It wasn't easy holding my mental and emotional composure in this situation due to my excitement, but I did the best I could, remaining as calm as possible in order not to cause an automatic return to my physical body. A voice from the darkness around us began speaking to me; although the man in the picture wasn't visibly doing any talking, it seemed as though the picture and the voice were somehow connected, as if the man was somehow speaking to me. The voice spoke of having a great feeling of love for me. I listened for maybe thirty seconds but finally my growing excitement about what was happening became too great. I lost control and shifted back inside my physical body.

Here the story continues and becomes even more of an adventure. I was about to start contemplating again when an unusual sensation in my feet and ankles distracted me. I began to realize a pair of hands was gently rubbing my feet and ankles, as if to calm and soothe me, massaging first one foot and ankle for a few seconds and then the other. Hardly believing this was happening, I still tried to remain perfectly motionless so as not to risk spoiling this exciting adventure. The touch of the two hands rubbing my feet and ankles felt so good that I didn't want this sensation to end, but focusing my attention on this gentle foot massage caused my physical body to gradually wake up. The touch of the two hands on my feet and ankles grew fainter and slowly faded away. I sneaked a peek through my eyelids to see who was at the foot of my bed, but couldn't see anyone in the darkness of my bedroom.

Wondering if the Master I'd seen in my inner experience was somehow responsible for this wonderful foot massage, I excitedly began chanting his name over and over while remaining motionless, trying to gradually drift into sleep. I was fully awake by now and my breathing was too short and jerky for me to fall asleep while chanting softly and slowly like this. Therefore I soon switched to the technique of listening to the faint high whistle in my head and drifted out of my body into blackness.

In this final experience of that night, I recall ending up in the same building that I'd been in earlier, during my first experience with the two ladies, but in a different room now. I met no one in this experience but felt a strange, unidentified force moving directly behind me which forcibly propelled me from one room in this large building to another, showing me different scenes and activities. I knew the force meant me no harm and therefore passively let it push me around the rooms. At one point I even tried testing the strength of the force by trying to place my feet solidly against the floor's surface, but the force ignored my ploy and kept pushing me onward to another room. I eventually

ended the experience by returning to my body, wondering at
all that had happened to me that night.

23

One Year after My First Out-of-Body Experience

These several months spent primarily on riverboats provided me with another valuable store of Soul Travel information. I was especially intrigued by my latest experiences. Even before this I'd begun to take a greater interest in the spiritual ideas put forth in Mr. Twitchell's books, but now I started seriously wondering about the existence of God, Spirit, and Soul, and particularly about the possibility of there actually being an all-powerful Godman who could somehow be with me during my inner travels.

After finally getting off the riverboats and heading back to the midwest to visit friends and relatives again, it took me two full weeks just to regain my normal sleep routine. When I finally resumed my nighttime contemplations, nothing happened for about a week. Then came another very special experience.

Visiting friends in Des Moines, I didn't feel well this particular evening because of a flu bug which apparently had me targeted as another victim. I woke up in the middle of the night with a fever and a very sore throat, and my plans for driving to Nebraska the next day to visit friends obviously cancelled.

While lying in bed feeling miserable and sorry for myself, I happened to remember a story in the book *In My Soul I Am Free* about how Paul Twitchell overcame a critical illness at a very young age. He was able to consciously leave his physical body for a short while, allowing a miraculous healing to take place. Curiously wondering if something like this could happen to me, I mustered all the will power within me to try to leave my body.

I began thinking of myself as a bodiless unit of awareness moving further and further out the top of my head into blackness, trying to let go all mental ties to the physical body and physical world. Being sick made it especially difficult to hold this thought pattern, and to keep from forgetting, I had to mentally remind myself over and over what I was trying to do. Finally, maybe forty-five minutes or an hour later, I drifted into sleep.

I was able to leave my body three times that night, for short intervals that I spent in an earthlike world with several other people present. I made the acquaintance and talked for awhile on two occasions with a fellow who was about my age, but twice I lost control and returned to my body instantly. Each time I returned, unable to tell how sick my physical body was or whether any miraculous healing had taken place, I exited again into the inner worlds. One time a very noticeable tingling sensation at a spot about two inches from the center of my head caught my attention, and I contemplated on it for awhile.

I was out for quite awhile the third time, and after returning to my body, curiosity got the best of me at this point. Anxious to see if any healing had taken place during my total time out of the body, I brought back all the physical senses. Lo and behold, my fever, nausea, sore throat, and head congestion, even my tiredness, were completely gone. Upon waking the next morning, the only trace of sickness in me was a slight sniffle, and I drove the several hundred miles to visit friends in Nebraska as planned. Similar Soul Travel healings have happened to me a number of times since then, but at the time I looked on this unexplainable healing as something of a miracle.

During the following week, I managed to leave my body a very encouraging number of nights using this same pattern of contemplation. These contemplation sessions of trying to "mentally go to blackness" weren't easy for me. After waking in the middle of the night it usually took a couple of hours of contemplating for me to drift into sleep. Most of these experiences were short, lasting only a few minutes, but the success gave me confidence and enthusiasm with each episode.

One of my contemplative sessions during this week deserves special mention here because of the real thrill it provided me. The movement out of my body happened so fast and so smoothly that my physical body didn't even have time to fall asleep. That night I ended up in a beautiful outdoor earthlike setting that looked something like a courtyard. I didn't have much chance to enjoy this situation, though. I inadvertently began to think about how easily I'd left my body with this new technique, and it caused a quick automatic return to my physical form.

Somehow I seemed to have established a pattern: whenever things got too easy, I'd get too excited and progress would come to a halt. And it had happened again. The reason for this unexpected turnabout of Soul Travel success was again my emotions of anticipation and apprehension which now began plaguing and disrupting my contemplations. Seeing this particular contemplative technique go flat on me was especially disheartening, because this time I'd felt so sure of having finally found a good, reliable one. Here it was, over a year since my first conscious trip out of the body, and I was still in the beginner stages, still struggling to find an answer to Soul Travel success, still searching for a reliable way of leaving my body.

24

Listening to the Sound Current

After this latest Soul Travel setback, instead of forging ahead, blindly trying different random contemplation techniques as I'd been doing for the past six months, I decided to pull back and take an overall objective look at the problem of my emotions interfering with my contemplation.

Assuming that it would always be difficult, if not impossible, for me to keep my emotions subdued during my contemplations, I thought I had just about two alternatives left to achieve any possible future Soul Travel success. Either I could give up on contemplation and go back to concentration or meditation, or I could try to find some pattern of contemplation which would enable me to leave my body automatically after drifting into sleep.

I decided to figure out something reliable to contemplate on, which wouldn't depend on my own conscious thoughts, yet would still enable me to move out of my body after slipping into sleep. Thinking back on all my previous concentration and contemplation attempts, only one consistency came to mind—hearing the faint high whistle in the top of my head. This sound had gradually gotten a little louder over the past year and was easier for me to hear. It only took maybe five minutes of contemplation for me to begin hearing the faint high whistle now. Paul Twitchell's books all spoke of this Sound Current as being vital with regard to out-of-body travel as well as life itself.

I decided to try contemplating strictly on this faint high whistle. After waking in the middle of the night, I would go back to sleep listening steadily to this sound in the top of my head, and to this new plan I decided to add one more twist. Contemplating in the middle of the night had thus far proven much more effective for me than at bedtime, for the simple reason that drifting into sleep while contemplating is easier and more of a certainty after waking in the middle of the night. I just needed to work on generating the needed desire to want to fully contemplate when I awoke, rather than falling back to sleep.

Here, then, was my new procedure. Just before bedtime I would read a few pages of one of my Soul Travel books and then just go to sleep. Either by alarm clock or self-suggestion, I would wake up in the middle of the night and go back to sleep, keeping my full attention on the faint high whistle in the top of my head. All thoughts concerning Soul Travel would be avoided while listening to this sound. Each time my mind wandered, I would simply bring it back and place my attention on listening to the sound again. If it took thirty minutes, or an hour, or three hours for me to drift into sleep, so be it. Any chance of moving out of my body, either automatically or of my own accord, would likely come at the moment of drifting into sleep—provided I was still listening to the faint high whistle in my head at that moment.

What to expect from this contemplative procedure I didn't know. But on the chance that this method did prove successful for me, the prospects for long term effectiveness and reliability seemed better from a Soul Travel technique such as this one. It was a simple, uncomplicated manner of contemplating, requiring minimal conscious thinking.

25

This Is the Godman

My very first attempt using this sound contemplation technique brought results, and they were interesting results, too. After reading a few pages of a Soul Travel book at bedtime and then going to sleep, I awoke in the middle of the night to focus all my attention on listening to the faint high whistle in the top of my head. I drifted into sleep while listening to the high whistle and became conscious that I was looking at a rather unusual color picture. All the pictures that had formed on my inner mind screen in the past had been motionless still-pictures. But this picture showed movement and activity, specifically a young man and young woman walking around inside what looked like a living room of a house here on earth.

Asleep physically, but now wide awake consciously, I was fascinated by this action-picture phenomenon. Equally interesting was the fact that I seemed to be a bodiless point of vision inside my physical head yet seemingly separate from my physical form. With a growing curiosity as to what I consisted of and what was happening, I slowly and carefully raised my inner vision above the picture and then below, to see if this action color scene would disappear. All the still-pictures that I'd witnessed on my inner mind screen in the past had been very delicate and would quickly disappear at the slightest break in attention, but this picture remained intact.

I gently focused my inner vision on this action color scene, drawing it closer and closer to my inner point of view; the people and objects began looking more and more lifesize and three-dimensional. Suddenly I felt a slight suction in the area of my Spiritual Eye and instantly found myself standing inside the picture.

The next night this same picture-phenomenon happened again. After waking in the middle of the night and contemplating on the faint high whistle for a couple of hours, I drifted into sleep and became aware of another action color picture on my inner mind screen. I easily moved into the picture and later managed to leave my body several more times this night.

With rising hopes for this new Soul Travel method, I continued using this same basic contemplation procedure during the following months and had good success with it; not great success, but good success. My notes show that over the next five months I consciously traveled out of the body about thirty different nights, which was a very respectable success percentage for me.

Part of these five months I spent staying with my brother in the midwest, waiting for another engine to be installed in my motor home. I had plenty of free time and contemplated an average of maybe two nights out of three. Having so much free time turned out to be very helpful to me. Neither this new contemplation technique nor the several other various sound-related contemplative techniques that I experimented with were easy for me.

I kept trying, kept experimenting, and kept learning. I began incorporating into all my contemplations the idea of avoiding any unnecessary conscious thoughts, especially all thoughts concerning Soul Travel. Doing this substantially reduced the disruptive effect of my emotions. These sound-related contemplative techniques were beginning to show me some degree of reliable effectiveness.

Once after being partially aroused from sleep in the early morning by my brother getting ready for work, I drifted back into a light sleep while listening to the high whistle in my head, and moved out of my body automatically just as my brother opened the front door of the apartment to leave for work. I was right behind him in my Soul body as he opened and closed the door in front of me. Wanting to follow him, I went right through the door. This would have been a fun adventure but I had difficulty mentally holding this out-of-body situation and a few seconds later shifted back inside my physical body again.

Of my out-of-body experiences during these months, several involved a force which bodily moved me around from one location to another. One experience resulted in a shift in energy levels, presumably a shift from one inner plane to another inner plane. Another time, everything around me suddenly turned white, and a tremendous surge of energy instantly penetrated the whole area as well as my inner body. Unable to withstand more than a few seconds of this almost-blinding white energy, I quickly lost control and returned to my body.

On a couple of occasions my out-of-body experiences resulted in sexual encounters with unfamiliar females. This was something new for me. My emotions usually became overstimulated, causing an automatic return to my physical body. But the kissing and body contact were just as real and arousing as if it had happened with my physical body. Later I came to realize that as Soul I had moved into my Astral body for these experiences, which occurred on the Astral Plane.

One night I traveled to perhaps the most beautiful city I've ever seen anywhere in any world. It had unusually narrow, paved streets and sidewalks lined with many small, colorful buildings built very closely to one another. Many people were walking around the downtown area of the city, so I started moving along one of the sidewalks, looking around trying to observe this beautiful scenery in detail. I wanted very much to be able to remember what these colorful, uniquely-styled buildings looked like. Unfortunately, I made the inadvertent mistake of hoping not to return to my physical body for awhile, and these thoughts of my physical form caused a quick automatic return. My mental reminder during this experience to look this unusual city over closely didn't help me recall more than a small portion of its striking scenery, but what I still can remember makes this the most memorable city I've ever seen anywhere.

Once when I was out of my body, I realized later that a noise outside the room where I was sleeping had aroused my conscious mind enough to cause me to be pulled back into my physical body automatically. Had the noise not occurred and not aroused my conscious mind, I would have returned from this out-of-body journey and awakened the next morning with no conscious memory whatsoever of having been out of the body during the night.

Another time while I was out of the body, I met three young girls who were sitting together in a small lighted area in the world of blackness, ages maybe six, eight, and ten; the bodies of these girls had the same visible appearance as the human body. My Astral body, in which I, as Soul, was traveling at that time, was solid, yet transparent and filled with many tiny white stars. A force slowly pushed me up to the three girls. I felt a tremendous amount of love for them and put my arms solidly around all three of them. The bond of love we all shared at this moment was beyond words. A few seconds later I returned to my body automatically.

It was during these five months that two noticeable changes took place in my dreams and my out-of-body experiences. Both of these changes started happening shortly after I began studying the personal discourses offered by Eckankar, the spiritual path that Paul Twitchell had written about. My dreams started becoming much more vivid and active, and my out-of-body experiences picked up speed. Both my leaving and returning now became instantaneous movements away from and back into my physical body.

My reason for studying the Eckankar discourses was to learn more about the Godman spoken of in some of the Soul Travel books that Paul Twitchell had written. The idea of such a man existing and having these capabilities intrigued and fascinated me. I was also ready to take the next step of having a guide for my somewhat random Soul Travel experiences.

Then about two months after beginning my study of the Eckankar discourses, I had an experience which involved this Godman. I was out of the body one night and happened to remember the Spiritual Master. Being in an outdoor earthlike environment with several other people, I asked them if they knew anything about the Living ECK Master, or where he could be found. Surprisingly, this time the answer was "yes."

One fellow led me to a large, modern building nearby where I could supposedly find this Godman. Maybe thirty seconds later the man I'd been asking for walked into the lobby area. He was dressed in a casual shirt and slacks, and after walking up to me and greeting me by name, he led me down a hallway to a small private room.

I felt rather humble and nervous being in the presence of this Godman and didn't feel brave enough to say much. But I didn't have to, for he took a chair across from me and began talking about spiritual matters. I just listened. A short while later, he asked me a question that I was reluctant to answer honestly, and I became a trifle flustered. The uncomfortable emotions caused a quick, automatic shift back into my physical body.

This was my only conscious out-of-body experience with the Living ECK Master during this five-month period, but several of my dreams involved him.

My thirty or so different successful Soul Travel nights during these five months resulted in two new ways of moving out of the body for me. One was the action-picture phenomenon, which happened to me about half a dozen times. In each case it was very easy to move into the

113

picture; these live, moving scenes were very durable and wouldn't easily disappear. The other new way of leaving my body happened twice and was totally different from anything I'd experienced before. Twice while contemplating I felt a powerful force tumbling me around inside my physical body. The first time this happened it was rather scary; it took a couple of seconds for me to realize that my inner body had been spun around and was separated from my physical body.

During these months I was also learning a great deal about contemplation. I learned that there was a best time for waking up in the middle of the night to contemplate; waking too early made it almost impossible for me to generate the needed desire to want to fully contemplate, and waking too late made it very difficult for me to drift back into sleep. I learned that the early morning was also a productive time of day for contemplating and moving out of my body.

I developed a new sound technique during this time, imagining the sound of the faint high whistle as a current of energy flowing into the top of my head and focusing on the tingling sensation that would develop at this particular spot. Somehow my chances of moving out of my body seemed improved when I did this.

By the end of this five-month period of learning, I still didn't have a specific pattern of contemplation that I used exclusively or was overly proud of, but for the first time I was seeing some degree of repeated success. Contemplation was still a long, arduous chore for me, though; it still usually took me at least an hour and a half and sometimes two hours of contemplating to even begin to travel out of the body, but my hopes were for continued improvement in the future.

Of the approximately thirty different nights during these five months that I did manage to consciously leave my body, about half a dozen of these experiences happened unexpectedly during sleep, without having fully contemplated beforehand; the other twenty to twenty-five

114

successful Soul Travel nights were earned the hard way, by contemplating long and hard either in the middle of the night or in the early morning. Many of these successful Soul Travel nights I was able to move out of the body more than once the same night, which resulted in many more exciting inner travels for me. It was always much easier contemplating, drifting into sleep, and moving out of the body a second or third or fourth time, etc., of any given night than it was getting out the first time.

26

A Scorecard of Patterns

B y the end of these five months, several obvious patterns had begun to surface. I will record them here because these same patterns may hold true for most other beginning Soul Travelers.

I'd learned the hard way that in any out-of-body situation, thoughts concerning my physical body would almost always cause an automatic return. Even thinking some innocent thought — such as I wonder how long I'll be able to stay out of body or I'm afraid I might return to my physical body soon — would almost always be followed by an automatic return to my physical form.

A second pattern that had shown up in my out-of-body travels had direct ties to this first tendency: the better my out-of-body conscious awareness, the shorter my experience usually was. The converse was also true. When my out-of-body conscious awareness was poor, I often didn't remember about my physical body and inadvertently kept it from being aroused from sleep.

A third pattern emerged: the better my out-of-body awareness, the better my conscious recall of the experience. However, having very good or excellent out-of-body conscious awareness seldom left me with perfect recall because, for some reason, I usually lost many of the details

117

immediately after reentering my physical body. Sleep and the passing of time generally robbed my memory even more. As a result, experiences which I could still remember half of the following morning were the exception and not the rule.

One other obvious and important pattern was that the more times I left my body in one night, the poorer my memory of these adventures; presumably this was because more experiences meant more details and activities for my memory to hold, which became increasingly difficult with each successive experience.

27

A Reliable Way of Leaving the Body

When major engine repairs were finally completed on my motor home, I started traveling again. This time I headed toward the southeast to do some sightseeing. Having plenty of free time and being able to sleep late in the mornings made it possible for me to contemplate most nights, and by experimenting with various sound-related contemplative techniques, my Soul Travel success gradually began to show some improvement. Encouragingly during this two-month tour through the southeastern states, I managed to leave my body twenty to twenty-five different nights.

Early on during this trip I made two changes in my contemplation procedure, one of these changes being especially helpful. By forcing myself to get up out of bed for just a minute or two in the middle of the night, splashing some water on my face to wake myself up, and also going to the bathroom, it was much easier for me to generate the needed desire to want to fully contemplate. I also began going back to bed and contemplating in a position lying on my back instead of in my normal sleeping position on my stomach. This seemed to prevent me from making only a halfhearted contemplative try.

Toward the middle of this two-month sightseeing trip a very special out-of-body experience occurred which involved the Spiritual Master spoken of in previous chapters.

During a Soul Travel experience, I became conscious of sitting alone on a park bench in a dimly-lit, grassy park. The sky above me was dark, almost black, the only light being provided by a lamppost. I decided to ask for this Living ECK Master I'd been studying about, so in a louder than normal voice said, "If you're here, please show yourself." No sooner had these words passed my lips than the figure of a man standing in the darkness about fifteen feet away startled me. I was positive that I had been alone only moments before! It took me a second or two to get over the shock of this man's mysterious appearance, and then I saw who he was. A tremendous wave of love and emotion flooded through me at this moment, even causing me to start crying. I stood up and walked over to him, putting one of my arms around him and speaking to him. We started walking away through the dimly lit park, but unfortunately, about this time I started worrying about maybe losing this special experience and returned quickly to my physical body.

After this memorable experience with the Spiritual Traveler, I started asking for him more and more during my inner travels, and during the last month of my southeasterly trip he showed up during quite a few of my nightly journeys. I didn't always remember to ask for him, and he didn't always make an appearance when I did, but nevertheless each of my experiences with this man was very exciting. I could never stay out of the body with him for very long, though. Each time he showed up during one of my inner travels, I would soon start hoping not to have to return to my physical body. Invariably thoughts like these would cause a quick return to my physical form.

Two of these half-dozen experiences with the Living ECK Master were unusual enough to mention.

Once while out of my body, I happened to think about this Adept while walking along a city sidewalk. In a casual tone of voice I asked outloud for him to show himself if he was nearby. Immediately he walked up from behind me and put his arm around my shoulder. Seeing this spiritual Adept walking beside me, I was amazed at how quickly he'd appeared. We talked for awhile, and then I returned to my physical body.

Another one of my experiences with this Master was even more unusual. While out of the body, I was inside a very large building in some inner world. I walked over and joined a group of about a dozen other people, who were standing in a wide hallway of this building; then remembering about the Master, I asked in a low inconspicuous voice for him to show himself if he was anywhere around. Moments later a nearby hallway door opened and in he walked. He addressed all of us briefly and then began leading our group down the long hallway.

As we all paraded past a door further down the hall something strange happened. To everyone in the group's surprise and amazement, the door opened and in walked another dozen or so exact duplicates of the spiritual Adept, each one joining our group. Now our group consisted of myself, about a dozen other people, plus about a dozen replicas of the Spiritual Master.

With very good conscious awareness in this situation I not only watched in awe as this happened, my curiosity began to grow as to what was going to happen next. Unfortunately, I didn't get a chance to find out. Before reaching the end of the long hallway, I again made the easy-to-make mistake of hoping not to return to my physical body for awhile, and these thoughts caused a quick automatic return.

Soon after this, the image of a blue star or stars began appearing to me. Once during sleep I became partially conscious of many small blue stars on my inner mind screen, and then a close-up image of a man appeared on the black inner screen. My suspicion was that I'd seen the Inner Master. This same phenomenon of blue stars and the Inner Master was described in my Eckankar discourses and some of my Soul Travel books. Another night I saw a large blue star on the inner screen and, by sleepily focusing on it, I managed to move out of my body, ending up in a lifelike environment with the Master.

Small tidbits of useful information were slowly gained during these months. I learned in my flying experiences how to fly a certain way to avoid flying into and becoming lost in the massive zone of blackness that existed above many of the inner lifelike worlds that I experienced. I started limiting my inner-world flights to within twenty feet or so of ground level to avoid flying into blackness and causing an automatic return to my physical form.

By the second month of this leisurely sightseeing trip, an interesting pattern had begun to develop in the length of my out-of-body experiences. Most of my initial experiences of any given night were turning out quite short, maybe only a few seconds or minutes. However, by going back to sleep and lightly contemplating on the high whistle, it was then relatively easy for me to move out of body again, maybe several more times the same night. These successive experiences usually lasted longer than my initial experience. The majority of my successful Soul Travel nights during these two months ended up with two or more out-of-body experiences the same night. This pattern of my first experience being short, but my second and third projections the same night being longer became rather common.

Toward the end of this two-month trip, I uncovered my most valuable bit of information to date about contemplation. I learned that the closer I let the black inner screen draw to my inner point of vision while contemplating, the better my chances were of moving out of the body after drifting into sleep. I also gradually began to notice that the direction my eyes were pointed during contemplation made a difference, too. Pointing my eyes straight ahead, instead of downward, seemed to be better. Doing some more experimenting with this idea, I tried lifting my inner vision upward while contemplating on the high whistle, trying to drift into sleep with my eyes pointed in an upward direction. The result was that my experiences out of the body became more frequent.

As my Soul Travel success improved, it soon became evident that I'd finally found a consistent and reliable way of leaving my body. The plan went like this. I would practice waking up in the middle of the night, getting out of bed for a couple of minutes, then going back to sleep. My primary attention was on keeping my eyes rotated upward as high as possible in my head yet staying relaxed; then I'd concentrate on listening to the faint high whistle in the top of my head. If I could drift into sleep still contemplating like this, my chances of moving out of my body automatically were very good. This technique showed me a high degree of effectiveness; for the first time I'd found a pattern of contemplation that did. Why it worked was a mystery to me, but the important and exciting thing was that it *did* work—consistently.

28

Let's Pause for a Moment

I f you've gotten this far in the book, then you must have a genuine interest in exploring the possibility of Soul Travel for yourself. I'm going to pause here and challenge your open-mindedness even more. In this chapter I'll discuss some different characteristics I've discovered about the inner worlds of which I've spoken so often. If you've not already consciously experienced and verified the existence of these inner worlds for yourself, perhaps this information will make these nonphysical universes seem a little more real to you.

1. Physical vs. Nonphysical

From what I understand, there are many different inner worlds; some exist within the realm of time, space, and matter, and some do not. All consist of a higher vibrational energy than the physical world that you and I know. In my own experiences I am most familiar with the worlds within the realm of time, space, and matter; my inner travels seem to land me on worlds just as solid, three-dimensional, and real as earth. Time doesn't seem to be of significance when I move into these lifelike inner worlds, but the dimension of time actually does exist there. Where there's movement from one location to another, there must be time.

But beyond the realm of time, space, energy and matter, still other worlds are said to exist; changeless eternal worlds said to be the true home of Soul. Soul resides there in Its true, bodiless, all-knowing, all-seeing, omnipresent state, and travels into the lower realms for the purpose of gaining spiritual experience.

For a long time the descriptions in my Soul Travel books had me visualizing the inner worlds stacked in layers, one on top of another, but I gradually began to understand this isn't the case. The physical universe has no outer boundaries and neither do the inner worlds. All worlds seem to occupy the same areas of space throughout all of space, each able to function independently of the other worlds because they are each vibrating at a different rate of energy. An inner plane spoken of as being higher or lower than another simply refers to a difference in vibration, not separation by linear distance.

The physical body and physical senses can't detect the presence of nonphysical worlds, but the different inner bodies inside the physical form can. Each inner body vibrates at a different rate of energy and serves as an outer protective covering for Soul within.

2. Earthlike or Non-Earthlike

"As above, so below" is a rather well-known phrase which simply means that everything existing in the physical world also exists in the inner worlds. The many different lifelike inner worlds within the realm of time, space, and matter are said to have all things found here on earth plus anything else imagineable.

Probably not more than five percent of my travels out of my body stretched my imagination this way, introducing me to inner worlds where there's no telling what might be seen. I stuck with mostly earthlike people and earthlike landscapes and buildings. But brief glimpses of outer-space-like terrains led me to believe that more unusual places do exist.

3. The Law of Gravity

As you might expect, the physical laws of nature aren't law in the inner worlds. A good example of this is the law of gravity. I can mentally neutralize the pull of gravity on my inner body at any time and become weightless. How this works, I don't fully understand, but all that's needed for me to fly or levitate myself in inner-world situations is to think about flying or levitating myself and then doing it; it's this simple.

4. Flying

The requirements for flying in the inner worlds are simple, straightforward, and easy: to want to fly, to think about flying, and then to actually do it, making sure to continue thinking about flying while in flight. Even the beginning Soul Traveler will find this easy to learn. Usually my inner-world flights are done with my arms outstretched like glider wings, but sometimes I point my arms straight out in front of me like Superman or fly with them down at my side.

During many of my inner-world flights I can feel a subtle buoyant force or power aiding my flight and varying my flying speed according to my thoughts. It could be that flying in the inner worlds is actually accomplished with the grace and assistance of an all-knowing higher power.

5. People

Most of the people I meet or see in the inner worlds are, in appearance, earthlike in every way, of varied ages and ethnic background. A small percentage of my experiences involve alien-looking creatures, which makes for some interesting encounters, but this doesn't happen too often.

Still puzzling to me is how I can travel out of the body with friends or relatives from this physical life. My suspicion is that many of these familiar individuals are somehow impersonated in the inner-worlds for my learning experience, but some may actually be who they appear to be.

I've also had a couple of interesting out-of-body encounters with deceased relatives from this physical life, but after returning to my body again I could only wonder about the authenticity of these relatives I'd seen or talked to.

6. Communication

Verbal communication between myself and other people in the inner worlds is always carried on in the English language. I would assume that most all Soul Travelers communicate in their own language in out-of-body situations. Mental telepathy is another fascinating way of communicating in the inner worlds, and it's something I've consciously experienced a number of times.

7. Mode of Dress

Generally the clothes I find myself wearing in the inner worlds are of contemporary styles but are not copies of the clothes from my own limited physical wardrobe.

During my first couple of years of Soul Traveling, a significant percentage of my out-of-body experiences involved a partial state of dress, but nowadays most of my inner ventures are done fully clothed. Finding myself totally nude while out of the body is rare for me; I can only recall a few cases of this happening.

8. Passing through Solid Objects

Here's another interesting phenomenon that can be done in the inner worlds. If I'm out of the body in some inner lifelike world and decide for some reason I want to pass through a wall or a door, all I have to do is this: I must want to pass through it, believe one-hundred percent that I can pass through it, and slowly extend my inner body into and through it. Sounds simple and easy, and it is—except for one thing: a 99.99% belief in success isn't good enough. Just a trace of doubt in my mind about not succeeding, and the wall or door will remain solid to my touch.

Passing through solid objects made of glass is different, because under certain conditions glass displays unusual characteristics in the inner worlds. If I'm not totally confident of my ability to move through the glass, it begins bending and stretching to the shape of the leg or arm which I'm trying to push into it. The bending glass may even make an eerie sound similar to the sound caused by physical fingers being rubbed across an inflated balloon. There's another interesting phenomenon that can happen. If while slowly extending myself into the bending and stretching glass, I stop thinking about trying to pass through the window, mentally give up so to speak, the bent glass will immediately become hard and brittle and shatter into countless tiny pieces. If I'm able to shed from my mind any last doubts about not succeeding, the bending surface of the glass will suddenly allow me to freely pass through it and then spring back to its original flat hard shape, intact and unbroken. It seems that my thought forms had a whole lot to do with what happened each time.

9. Pain

During my first two years of Soul Traveling I only experienced a couple of instances of pain in out-of-body situations, both of these occurring while inadvertently shifting from one inner plane to another of higher vibration. I gradually began to wonder if it was even possible to hurt my inner bodies in an out-of-body situation, since I always emerged unscathed even from the most reckless of my adventures.

Then one night something interesting happened which proved to me that my Astral body can feel pain. I carelessly flew too high above the ground and suddenly found myself enveloped by a world of blackness. Quickly becoming disoriented, I thought that I must have returned to my physical body, and I stopped concentrating on my flying. The next thing I knew I was crashing to the ground of an inner-world, falling like a rock, and hitting the ground about as hard and as painfully as if I'd fallen a distance of ten or fifteen feet in this physical world. The pain from this fall stayed with me for several seconds but I suffered no real damage to my Astral body.

10. Fear

Fear is such a basic ingredient of Soul Travel for some people that I want to discuss this topic in three separate categories: (1) fear of leaving the body, (2) fear of being out of the body, and (3) scary out-of-body situations.

a) Fear of leaving the body

In a wide-awake, fully conscious state I'm still afraid of leaving my body, always have been and probably always will be. Soul Travel success for me comes from what I do best, contemplating and drifting into an early stage of sleep and then moving out of my body. Using this procedure, I can neutralize my conscious fears of leaving my body since I am not wide awake at the moment I leave it.

b) Fear of being out of the body

Becoming more accustomed to the sensation of being in an inner body gradually erases this fear. It took me six months to a year after my very first conscious movement out of the body for my fear of being separated from my physical form to fade away.

c) Scary out-of-body situations

I've learned a great deal these past several years about how to react in threatening out-of-body circumstances. I've learned that nothing can harm me while I'm out of my body. No scary out-of-body experience has ever caused me any harm or pain.

During the past several years I've learned three different ways to neutralize any threatening or frightening out-of-body situation. First, if threatened or bothered by some other creature or person in some inner lifelike world, I can become totally passive, and the threatening creature or person will then become passive as well. Second, I can turn the tables and become the aggressor myself. I can recall a number of instances of punching bothersome people or creatures to let them know that I don't have to put up with their fear tactics, and some of the surprised facial expressions I've seen after these punches have been classics, especially in cases of hitting some creature several times my own size. A third easy way of overcoming any threat in an out-of-body situation is to simply say outloud, "In the name of God, be gone!" This simple command will cause the threat to either vanish instantly or to become passive and nonaggressive.

The key to overcoming a scary out-of-body situation is to constantly remember that nothing can harm you.

Hopefully the information in this chapter has been interesting to you, whatever your reaction to it. Now to continue with my own story.

29

The Transparent Guide

An interesting change had gradually surfaced in my attitude toward Soul Travel; I'd not only become much less talkative about my own inner experiences, but also about Soul Travel in general. Out-of-body travel had become a common, everyday part of my life by now, and the urge to enlighten the world to this reality wasn't nearly as compelling within me as in months past. Certainly I still enjoyed discussing this topic with other people, but now in a more guarded way, and only with more open-minded, genuinely interested individuals.

I was back on the riverboat by now, my work-sleep schedule keeping my Soul Traveling time to a minimum. But I still experienced some dozen unexpected trips out of the body during this period of time. Several turned out to be rather unusual or special in some way.

One night, after a noise disturbed my sleep, I woke up in the Soul form and saw a swirling red picture on my inner screen. It quickly formed into a scene of distant planets set against black space, then zoomed in on one of the planets which I recognized as earth. The picture changed to a close-up, map-like view of the continents of North and South America and gradually focused on one small area of Canada which looked to be in the vicinity of Winnipeg, Manitoba.

A fleeting intuitive thought flashed by that this area had something to do with a past life of mine.

Another evening an unexpected minor healing occurred. A contact lens problem had caused a slight infection in one of my eyes, and it was sore that night at bedtime. I fell asleep and became conscious of being out of my body in an inner lifelike world. I consciously moved out of my body a second time later that night, and upon awaking to go to work I noticed that my sore eye was completely healed. Such infections usually required at least a couple of days to heal, but this one was cleared up overnight.

One night when I was feeling somewhat sick, I woke to find a current of energy flowing through my physical body, funneling into the top of my head and exiting out my feet. It felt something like electricity and the increasing intensity of this current of energy woke me up mentally, although my physical body remained asleep. It rushed through me like a powerful flood of water, seemingly cleansing my physical body. As this was happening, I knew instinctively that this current flowing through me had a potential strength far beyond what I was now receiving, far beyond anything I could even imagine. As the seconds passed, this energy current flowing through me slowly began to subside, and within another five seconds or so had faded away altogether. I went back to sleep feeling much better physically, and upon awaking an hour or so later for work, my earlier signs of sickness were completely gone.

Working for three months straight on the riverboat seemed like an eternity, but I survived. After finally getting off the boat, I drove south towards the warmer climates. It took a couple of weeks just to regain my normal sleep routine, and it wasn't until several weeks later that I started seriously contemplating again at night. I resumed my middle-of-the-night contemplations and went back to using the same contemplative technique that had been effective for me several months earlier, that of listening to the faint high whistle in my head. In a few days I was regularly moving out of my body again. I soon started doing some experimenting with the technique and came up with another very helpful contemplative change.

It was very difficult for me to keep my eyes pointed upward until drifting into sleep, so I began rotating my eyes upward only for the first thirty or forty-five minutes of contemplation, then allowed my eyes to drop downward to a normal relaxed position, keeping my inner vision pointed slightly upward until eventually drifting into sleep. It was primarily my inner vision that mattered, it turned out. I also began experimenting with sound, thinking of the high whistle as music putting me to sleep, or imagining the high whistle as a current of energy flowing through my body. Some of these different contemplative combinations showed more promise than others, but unfortunately none proved short, simple, and easy. Contemplating in the middle of the night still remained a long and difficult two-hour chore for me, even at this point.

With a resumption of my Soul Travel adventures at a rate of about one successful Soul Travel night out of three, it didn't take long for my enthusiasm and confidence to return to full strength again. During the first month and a half of this three-month trip to the south-southeast, I managed to leave my body about a dozen or fifteen different nights, most of these successful Soul Travel nights ending up as two or more out-of-body experiences the same night, and sometimes as many as six or eight. As always, my first experience in any given night was the tough one; successive experiences the same night were always much easier to achieve.

Several of my Soul Travel experiences at this time included the Inner Master. I still wasn't able to stay out of the body with him for very long, maybe a few minutes at most. I also had a couple of inner encounters with friends or relatives from this physical life, and on one occasion I ended up out of the body in the physical environment. The rest of my experiences all ended up in the inner worlds.

One night an interesting thing happened that somehow caused an overlapping of the inner and physical worlds for a moment. I was in an earthlike environment and found myself in a hot and heavy kissing session with an attractive young lady. Getting my emotions all steamed up caused me to lose control and return instantly to my body. I was surprised to still be able to feel the somewhat faint sensation of a pair of lips actively kissing me.

Around the middle of the three months I spent on my driving trip, another of my monumental Soul Travel experiences occurred. One night while flying in my inner body, I remembered the Spiritual Master and called his name. Immediately a force behind me changed the direction of my flight by applying a light pressure on the bottom of my feet. I looked behind me to see what had changed my course and saw a young man I'd never seen before. He was nice-looking, maybe thirty to thirty-five years of age, six feet tall, medium-length brown hair, and was dressed in blue jeans and a red and white checked lumber shirt. Here's the next shocker—he was transparent! Flying along with his arms outstretched and his hands gently cupped around my heels, every detail of this fellow's appearance was clearly visible, but I could also see through him.

Seeing this unfamiliar young man was a truly spectacular sight, momentarily holding me in a state of disbelief. My first excited impulse was to let this fellow know I'd seen him. He wasn't looking at me, though; he was studying the ground below and didn't even know I'd spotted him. I shuffled my feet back and forth in his hands a couple of times which made him look up. He released my feet and casually waved at me, then pointed toward the ground. I made the assumption that he meant for me to fly down there in order to find the Spiritual Master. I nodded my head and waved back and then dove downward toward the ground in the direction he'd pointed. Once on the ground, I asked several people if the Living ECK Master was anywhere around, but the answer was no.

A short sequel to this story is that a couple of months later I met and recognized this same young man during another out-of-body experience. He told me he'd meant for me to fly to a different place on the ground than I had. Maybe the Master would've been there.

30

A Piece of the Puzzle Fits

T his remarkable experience of discovering the fellow
flying behind me set the wheels of my mind in
motion. I became convinced that during other past out-of-
body travels there'd been a person flying behind me.
Instances of being bodily moved around from one location
to another in past inner-world situations also gave clues that
the mysterious force behind me may well have been a person. The force had usually lifted me as if there'd been a
hand on each side of my hips.

Now that the cat was out of the bag, a host of other questions sprung up. Who were these people behind me during
some of my inner experiences? What were their motives?
How did they know about me or know where to find me?
Were these people associated with the Inner Master in some
way? How did they get behind me so discreetly?

Now Soul Travel had become even more intriguing. An
important piece of the Soul Travel puzzle had fit into place,
but now the puzzle was much larger than before. I was
eagerly looking forward to learning some of the answers to
these questions.

31

Who's Flying Behind Me?

Two Years and Two Months after
My First Out-of-Body Experience

T he last half of this three-month trip to the southeastern United States was packed full of exciting out-of-body adventures. I'll include just a sample in this section.

The next time I found myself flying while out of my body, I noticed again a subtle force behind me seemingly pushing me through the sky. I curiously turned my head to see, but the only thing visible against the dark sky was a fuzzy, transparent outline of a person's body, maybe twice the size of mine. I reached back and tried touching it to see what it consisted of, and my hand passed through it. Within its outline was a very noticeable feeling of high energy. I reached back to where my feet were and felt a solid pair of hands gently cupped around my feet. I moved myself to a sitting position on top of these two hands, letting the person or thing behind me do the flying. Enjoying myself very much by now, I reached down and took hold of the solid hands beneath me, squeezing them several times in a friendly manner. The hands squeezed back. I assumed this being was a person, maybe the Inner Master, but I was drawn back into my physical body soon after, so I didn't find out.

141

The next visit to the inner worlds was practically the same; a buoyant force held me up from below. Again a solid pair of invisible hands were gently fitted around my feet! I reached back and took hold of the two solid hands and pulled myself up into a midair position, sitting on top of them; then in a rather brash and cocky manner, proceeded to point in the direction of where I wanted to fly. Whenever I wanted the guiding force to change directions, I simply pointed in whatever direction I wanted to go and the force obeyed.

During the coming weeks this strange phenomenon of flying with the two solid hands molded around my feet became rather common for me, and gradually a pattern began to develop. Usually when flying out of my body through a world of blackness, I could count on a high-energy, transparent form to be flying behind me, the hands being the only part of the silhouette to be touching me. I also began to sense an invisible presence with me, even when I wasn't flying or moving at all. Once I saw a young lady flying behind me, but when I tried to ask her questions about who she was, she wouldn't give me any answers. A short time later I lost control and returned to my body automatically, just as puzzled as before about these guides who traveled with me.

Sometimes these beings would appear as colors, or silhouettes of high energy. Sometimes they were blue or yellow, and could resolve into solid forms. Once an invisible being grabbed my arms from behind and then changed into the Inner Master. With a big, wide grin on his face, he said, "Pull up a chair and this time stay awhile." Very excitedly I chatted with him for maybe five full minutes (longer than usual) before returning to my body automatically.

One time the guide was a young Negro man. Another time I saw a short, pudgy, bald-headed man of maybe fifty years old, who was wearing glasses. Looking at me in a rather confused and embarrassed manner when I asked what he was doing, he started stammering something about being sent to assist me as a "transporter."

I remained very curious, even after this experience, as to who were these people flying behind me in the inner worlds. However I learned very little about them. Despite talking with a number of these people for awhile, very few of my questions got answered, either because they were reluctant to answer them, their answers didn't make sense to me, or because I often forgot what I had heard. About the only bit of consistent information that I received and remembered was that at least some of these individuals knew about Eckankar and the Living ECK Master.

One night I was actually pulled out of my physical body. This was a new experience to me: I felt someone taking hold of the hands of my inner body and pulling me gently out of my physical body into blackness. In front of me appeared a picture showing a side view of the Inner Master. He was moving slowly through a crowd of people, greeting them. I ended up moving into a room where the Inner Master was talking to a man dressed in a bright red robe. A very noticeable tingling sensation at a certain spot on the top of my head distracted me at this point. Reaching up, I curiously touched this spot with one of my fingers. Unfortunately, touching this tender spot caused a quick, unexpected shift back into my physical body.

I used this spot in another inner adventure, which turned out to be very important to me even though the importance wasn't apparent until many months later. I was flying on the heels of a ferocious inner wind, of a velocity of maybe eighty miles per hour. Finally achieving some flight stability, I put my attention on this spot on my head and mentally induced a slight feeling of tightness. All at once the strong winds began rushing through me as well as past me, pouring through this particular spot on top of my head and through my entire body with tremendous speed and force.

Experiencing this sensation of very strong winds was indescribably fantastic, but something important happened during this experience which I didn't pay much attention to at the time. Allowing the powerful rush of wind into and through my inner body caused a small hole to open up on top of my head there. It remained open, but not for a long time did I begin to understand the sigificance of it, which I'll discuss later.

It was about this time that an interesting change began taking place in my relationship with the Inner Master; during many of my inner travels I remembered about him but didn't ask for him to show himself, purposely. Realizing that if he visibly showed up, I probably wouldn't be able to stay out of body with him for very long, I chose instead to try to remain out of body as long as possible, content to do other things in the inner worlds. I still ended up seeing the Master during quite a few of my experiences, and each of my inner encounters with him was special; but I began to realize that being face-to-face with the Inner Master wasn't necessary for me, at least not at this point in my Soul Travel career. Knowing that he was always with me, always aware of my thoughts and activities, always assisting me in various ways, was far more important.

Towards the end of this three-month vacation I made another small but helpful change in my technique which made contemplation a little easier and less time-consuming for me. While listening to the high whistle during my contemplations, I had been thinking of this sound as a current of energy flowing into my body through the top of my head and flowing out of my feet. I reversed this process and imagined that it flowed upward through my physical body and out the top of my head at that certain spot I mentioned earlier. A slight feeling of tightness would oftentimes develop at that spot when I did this, and by keeping my secondary attention on this slight feeling of tightness, my chances of moving out of the body were improved for some reason. Doing this helped to lift my inner vision upward in a much more relaxed way.

144

Making this one small contemplative change reduced my average contemplation time at nights to about two hours, instead of two and a half hours or more, and also increased my chances of successfully traveling out of my body to about sixty percent, which was outstanding for me.

32

Two Soul Travel Techniques

Here's a more detailed description of this contemplation technique that was giving me such good results. My preparation for travels out of the body consisted of certain steps. First, I chose my time carefully. I seldom tried this technique on a night when I had to wake up early the next morning because of the length and difficulty of this contemplation method. On a good night, just before going to bed, I would read a few pages of some Soul Travel book, to turn my thoughts toward the inner worlds. This helped strengthen my desire to want to fully contemplate after waking up in the middle of the night.

I would then go to bed and go to sleep as usual. Either by self-suggestion or the alarm clock, I would wake up in the middle of the night or early morning. The best wake-up time for me varied; usually I allowed myself about fifty to sixty percent of my normal sleep time before waking up. This left me tired, but hopefully not too tired to want to fully contemplate.

After waking up, I would force myself to get out of bed for a couple of minutes and splash some water on my face and go to the bathroom. This cleared my mind and helped me generate the needed desire to want to fully contemplate. I would go back to bed and begin contemplating in a position lying on my back. Here's the method I used the most:

Contemplation Technique A

With eyes closed, take a couple of minutes to relax the whole body, then rotate the eyeballs upward, far enough to cause a slight strain on the muscles around the eyes. This points the inner vision toward the forehead; then focus it on the black inner screen. Do not try to drift into sleep at this point, just try to keep the attention focused in this manner. Whenever the mind wanders, simply retrieve it and start over again. Listen for a faint high whistle in the top of the head, and place a secondary attention on listening to it.

Think of the high whistle as a sound current flowing upward through the physical body and out the top of the head at a certain spot about two inches just in back of the top center. Let the sound lift the inner vision upward in a relatively natural way. Gently stop focusing the inner vision on the blackness of the inner screen; doing this any longer can prevent sleep. Instead just keep a vague peripheral awareness at about the location of the Spiritual Eye in the inside of the forehead, in order to keep the black screen close to the inner point of vision. Eventually you will slip unsuspectingly into sleep.

If a slight tingling sensation or feeling of tightness develops at that certain spot in the head, so much the better. If not, that is okay too. Chances of moving out of the body after drifting into sleep are a little better if you induce and keep the secondary attention on this spot.

Even if this contemplative technique sounds relatively simple and easy, it wasn't for me at all. Very seldom did any type of contemplation go smoothly for me, mainly because of my mind's incessant wanderings. Having to retrieve my wandering mind again and again wasn't easy. One trick that I did find helpful was to mentally repeat over and over to myself what I was trying to do.

The toughest part of this contemplative technique usually comes after about an hour and a half into it. A seductive wave of mental and physical tiredness would sweep through the body, sorely testing mental toughness

148

and determination. Giving in to this tempting wave of tiredness and just going to sleep usually reduces any chances of consciously moving out of the body to near zero. Try to mentally rise above this wave of tiredness and continue contemplating; at this point your chances of traveling out of the body with good conscious awareness slowly improve with each passing minute.

Contemplation Technique B

A somewhat easier version of contemplation technique A just described is to skip the initial thirty to forty-five minute routine of keeping the eyes rotated slightly upward and the inner vision focused on the black inner screen. Everything else about this contemplation technique, technique B, is the same as contemplation technique A.

Both technique A and technique B took me a couple of hours each. The advantage of contemplation technique B is that it is somewhat less mentally and physically tiring than technique A. However, for me, this was offset by the disadvantage of its being only about half as effective due to the increased chances of falling asleep too soon and making only a halfhearted contemplative try.

33

My Most Important
Soul Travel Discovery

Throughout the next year, working on and off the riverboats and traveling the rest of the time to visit friends and family, my out-of-body travels continued with unexpected frequency. I also made a few important discoveries about Soul Travel, the Inner Master, and how to make my contemplative time more productive.

Some of my short bedtime contemplations involved listening to the faint high whistle in my head and keeping my inner vision pointed slightly upward, some were trial and error where I experimented with different techniques. I began using a chanting technique suggested in my Eckankar discourses which involved slowly and softly chanting some sacred word over and over for thirty minutes at bedtime. I gained a surprising number of unexpected conscious out-of-body experiences this way. This was a lot easier than some of the earlier techniques I had developed by trial and error and used successfully.

The topic of Soul as an individual unit of knowingness, capable of being everywhere at the same time and knowing all things, was a new concept to me that was discussed in one of my monthly Eckankar discourses. I went to bed contemplating this one night and found myself in a place where my mental powers were seemingly unlimited. I even thought to myself at the time, Hey, I know everything about everything. It was a strange sensation: I was still me, an individual unit of identity capable of tremendous powers of thought and knowledge, yet I seemed to consist of nothing. This unexpected conscious experience lasted only a matter of seconds before I lapsed back into sleep, and the next morning my conscious mental abilities were just as limited as before.

One night while on a riverboat, I went to bed and began practicing the chanting technique. Lying in a totally relaxed, near-sleep state, a deep humming sound became audible in the back of my head. It vibrated from a certain spot near the back of my head, and I became conscious all of a sudden, out of my body in an inner lifelike world. A very noticeable tingling sensation on top of my head caught my attention, and I reached up to touch a moderately strong column of energy, which was funneling downward through the open hole just behind the top center of my inner body head. I wondered if this was caused by or connected to the humming sound that had started while I was chanting earlier.

I later practiced this technique of imagining the column of energy passing through my head and it seemed to help me stay out of my body for longer periods of time. It was especially helpful to concentrate on this tingling sensation in my head whenever I wanted to delay returning to the physical body.

I had several inner experiences with the Inner Master during this time. Once a very clear, distinct voice began speaking to me, not through my ears but from inside my head. Recognizing the Living ECK Master's voice, I listened for about a full minute. He'd been flying behind me in an earlier episode and had not allowed me to fly where I wanted to. I wondered about this and he explained several things to me about what I had been experiencing lately.

In another incident, I found myself flying through a light blue sky with the Inner Master and an exact duplicate of myself. The Master, being in the lead, flew to the ground of a semi-earthlike world, and my duplicate and I followed. Standing a few feet away from my replica, I was so intrigued by seeing a perfect likeness of myself that I walked over and touched this other fellow and then studied him closely, trying to figure out how this could be. I curiously asked him if he was me which brought a big grin to his face, a nod of his head. The Master was standing a short distance away, paying no attention to what this fellow and I were doing, leaving me to figure this situation out for myself. The only thing I could think of as an answer for this phenomenon was that I may have somehow been operating with two of my inner bodies instead of just one.

Probably my most important and helpful Soul Travel discovery during this one year time-span was learning how to move out of the body more than once in the same night. The majority of my successful Soul Travel nights prior to this time had ended up as two or more experiences out of the body the same night, but during this year I figured out an even easier, simpler, more reliable way to move out of the body a second and third and fourth time, etc., the same night. After learning how to do this, there were some nights when I managed to leave my body as many as ten or fifteen times in a row.

This procedure for traveling out of the body more than once on any given night is so simple and easy that even a beginning Soul Traveler should be able to use it effectively. I'm going to describe how it is done in the next chapter. I'm not saying the first conscious movement out of the body is easy to achieve; it's the second and third and fourth successive experiences that are the goal of my new technique and can be useful to anyone, the veteran or the inexperienced Soul Traveler.

34

How to Leave the Body
Again This Night

My foolproof way of traveling out of the body auto-matically a second time or more the same night has only one guideline. Say you've already successfully gotten out once that night and want to try it again. All that's needed is to remain absolutely, perfectly motionless inside the physical body and drift back into sleep. It's okay to lightly swallow if need be, but no other part of the physical body should be moved. Sometimes the physical body will feel somewhat numb and uncomfortable, but if you can fall asleep again remaining perfectly motionless, it's very likely that you'll be able to move out of the body again automati-cally; at least it was true for me.

Regardless of what Soul Travel technique I used to gain my first out-of-body experience of any given night, or how long my first experience lasts, whether one second or two hours, I can use this same procedure to leave my body again and again the same night.

Sounds like a simple, easy way to travel out of the body more than once the same night, and it is, except for the two very important details that need further explaining.

First, as mentioned, after returning my physical body will oftentimes feel numb and uncomfortable. After two or more consecutive experiences, I'll often have to move my physical body to a more comfortable position in bed to be able to fall asleep again. Once my physical body has been moved, even slightly, I have to start over again, contemplating in some manner with a moderate amount of determination which will take some time, maybe thirty or forty-five minutes.

A second very important detail regarding this simple method of moving out of the body several times the same night has to do with out-of-body conscious awareness. Having good or very good out-of-body awareness is what makes Soul Travel fun and exciting. But I seem to lose this ability to remember my journeys when I use this successive technique. In order for me to have good out-of-body awareness, I have to lightly contemplate in some way while remaining motionless, waiting to drift back into sleep.

Here's a somewhat typical Soul Travel night for me that may help explain all of this a little more clearly.

Assuming I've contemplated in the middle of the night and drifted into sleep and somehow moved out of my body, I'm often drawn back into my physical body automatically after my experience is over. I lie in bed musing over this first experience, remaining absolutely motionless, and usually go back to sleep, lightly contemplating in some manner. Maybe ten minutes later, after drifting into sleep, I'm suddenly conscious of being out of my body again in another lifelike world. This can repeat itself over and over, until my physical body has become so numb and uncomfortable that in order for me to fall asleep again, I have to shift positions in bed.

Hopefully this example can be useful and informative to other beginning Soul Travelers.

35

Try These Contemplation Techniques

Three Years and Four Months after
My First Out-of-Body Experience

I n this chapter I want to describe a few more exciting experiences in my out-of-body travels that were happening during this period in my study of Soul Travel. Then I'll give you some new contemplative techniques to try for yourself.

I spent four of the next six months working on riverboats again, and another month visiting friends and family in the midwest, so I didn't have a chance to do much middle-of-the-night contemplating during this time. In spite of this, I still managed quite a few conscious out-of-body experiences, though most of these were the result of some good contemplative techniques I had been learning.

A couple of my inner travels during this six-month period included witnessing the Inner Master materialize instantly, which was rather spectacular. While out of body, flying with very good conscious awareness above a lighted lifelike environment, I reached out one of my arms and in a challenging tone of voice asked outloud for the Master to show himself if he was present. Instantly a solid hand clasped my outstretched hand, the Master suddenly materializing into a solid form flying beside me.

The transparent guides as well as the Inner Master were still helping me with my flying technique, cupping my heels as I flew, to guide me through the air. They also visited me as I was trying to get out of the body; twice I felt myself literally carried out of my physical body by two forms, gently holding my inner body by the hips.

I also had the experience of being out of the body while asleep inside my motor home, suspended in midair in a weightless inner body with full conscious awareness. My vision was slightly blurred but still good enough for me to see some of the inside furnishings of my motor home though the dim light. Sitting in midair next to me was a bluish, transparent shape of part of a person's form.

Instinctively feeling that this bluish person sitting next to me wasn't the Inner Master and not having a logical explanation for why he was there, I took the friendly lead and said in a voice which sounded exactly like my physical voice, "Is your name such-and-such?" I believed I knew this person's name because of mentally having picked up a certain unfamilar name during the dream I'd been having earlier. The figure responded, "Yes." I asked the bluish person his age, and the response was a short and crisp, "Twenty-one." I asked, "Do you want to come back to the physical world?" As if he was reluctant to answer me, he hesitated and then gave one word: "Yes." My next remark was, "I thought the inner worlds were supposed to be much more beautiful than the physical world." He made the statement that each person's world is created within that person; an explanation that made sense but seemed to contradict his notion of wanting to return to the physical world. It was an interesting experience for me.

Soul Travel became somewhat easier for me for some reason during these six months. My desire to contemplate for long periods of time in the middle of the night had begun to wane by this time, so I did some experimenting with various simple, relaxed contemplation techniques. I was actively searching for less time-consuming, less difficult

158

ways of leaving my body; and practically all my experiments yielded some degree of out-of-body success. Even my halfhearted contemplative tries and my short thirty minute sessions on the riverboats resulted in a fair percentage of conscious out-of-body experiences. Apparently because of learning by habit or practice, Soul Travel was finally becoming more simple and not as much work.

Since some of the contemplative techniques that I experimented with during this six-month period turned out to be reasonably effective for me, I'm going to describe several of them here. For all of these techniques, the steps prior to contemplation are the same as those described in chapter 32.

Contemplation Technique C

This is basically the same simple, uncomplicated contemplation technique that I'd used a couple of years earlier, of listening to the faint high whistle in the top of my head.

After getting out of bed for a couple of minutes in the middle of the night, I would go back to bed lying in a position on my back, take a few minutes to relax my whole body, and when the faint high whistle became audible inside my head, I would place my full attention on listening to this sound. Maybe fifteen or thirty minutes later I would then roll over onto my stomach in my normal sleeping position and continue listening to the high whistle until eventually slipping unsuspectingly into sleep. Contemplation went smoothly for me with this technique when I was able to stay relaxed and hold my emotions to a minimum.

One small but very helpful change that I added to this contemplation method was to mentally remind myself over and over to keep listening to the sound in the top of my head. Without doing this, I would soon forget, slip out of the technique, and fall asleep.

Contemplation Technique D

After getting up in the middle of the night I would go back to bed lying in my normal sleeping position and place my primary attention on relaxing the muscles across both my temples, from about the middle of the eyebrow to about an inch above the ear. Keeping my primary attention on relaxing these muscles, my secondary attention was directed toward relaxing the muscles around my eyes and the muscles across my eyebrows, and also listening to the faint high whistle in the top of my head. Sometimes I imagined the sound as a current of energy flowing upward through my physical body, through the muscles across both my temples, thinking of the sound as helping to relax my temple-area muscles.

This particular contemplation technique could prove to be a dark horse for some beginning or prospective Soul Travelers. The major drawback to this technique is that it's especially vulnerable to those two troublesome emotions of anticipation and apprehension. Keeping the muscles across both temple areas fully loose and relaxed is very difficult to do when these two bothersome emotions become persistent.

Contemplation Technique E

This is a chanting technique that I learned about from my Soul Travel books and Eckankar discourses and adapted to my own style of contemplating.

Lying in a position on my back, I would close my eyes, relax my body, and begin slowly and softly chanting some sacred word over and over. Any number of chanting words are suggested in my Eckankar reading material, but HU is the word I usually used, HU being another name for God which is relatively easy to chant. Taking in a big breath of air, I would softly and slowly say outloud, H-U, in a long, drawn-out manner. While slowly exhaling, I would sing each letter separately, drawing them together in the middle. I'd then take a short breath of air and exhale, and then another deep breath of air and repeat this same chant.

I gradually found that the best way for me to stay fully relaxed and fall asleep while chanting was to think of my voice as vibrating throughout my body, especially through my hands, wrists, feet, and ankles. When I kept my attention focused primarily on this vibrating tingling feeling, it was easier to chant myself to sleep.

From hindsight I can look back and say that this chanting technique may well have enabled me to achieve my very first conscious trip out of the body. There's the added advantage that chanting outloud like this can help keep the mind from wandering. Chanting silently won't usually stop the mind's wanderings, but in my experience chanting softly outloud will.

Contemplation Technique F

This contemplation technique is one I haven't mentioned yet. I used it regularly for awhile; it works with the imaginative faculty.

After taking a couple of minutes to relax my body, I would begin imagining the exact feeling of having just returned to my physical body from an out-of-body experience. This feeling I'm talking about is a tingling sensation throughout my body, the same kind of tingling sensation that's felt when a wave of chills sweeps through the body. I could do it by focusing my attention specifically on a tingling sensation in my hands, wrists, feet, and ankles.

The reason for this technique's effectiveness is that by mentally trying to simulate the tingling feeling that's felt after returning from a Soul Travel journey, the vibration level of my body can gradually be raised enough for my inner body to become my dominant outer body.

36

A Couple of Suggestions

I f you do happen to be a person interested in trying to experience conscious out-of-body travel, I want to offer a couple of suggestions at this point.

First, whatever Soul Travel technique you decide to try, whether from this book or various other Soul Travel books and resources, don't be surprised if you have trouble achieving that first conscious out-of-body experience. That is common for most people and I suggest trying your Soul Travel method in the middle of the night. This certainly isn't meant to imply that a future Soul Travel career needs to be built around a middle-of-the-night contemplation schedule; all I'm saying here is that those tough-to-achieve first few conscious experiences out of the body may come a little easier for you in the middle of the night rather than during the day or at bedtime.

Try the pre-contemplation steps listed in chapter 32 of this book. Read a few pages of some Soul Travel book (any of the basic Eckankar study books works well) just before bedtime. Then go to sleep in the usual way, but wake up and get out of bed for a couple of minutes in the middle of the night. Splash some water on your face or go to the bathroom, then go back to bed and try your Soul Travel exercise. If you sleep with someone, you'll probably find it best to go back to sleep in a different bed, in a dark, quiet room, so your mental efforts won't be disturbed by your sleeping partner. Any movement by a person sleeping next to you can sometimes cause an automatic return to your physical form if you do manage to move out of your body.

If you're a newcomer to Soul Travel your chances of success could be several times greater this way. Remember to get up out of bed for a couple of minutes, though; just waking up isn't good enough no matter how wide awake you seem to be. You may have to experiment with the time that you wake up in the night or early morning. As I mentioned in chapter 32, the best wake-up time is often when you're tired enough to fall back to sleep but not too tired to to force yourself out of bed for a minute or two.

It's also important for you to realize there are more ways to travel out of the body than there are people here on earth. Soul Travel techniques described in the various Eckankar books can play an important role in getting a person started on the path of Soul Traveling consciously. Gaining your first few conscious experiences out of the body will probably be easier using and relying on someone else's Soul Travel methods. But don't be afraid to experiment and develop your own Soul Travel techniques. Discovering what Soul Travel methods work best for you may take some time and require some effort and sacrifice.

If you're able to successfully use any of the contemplation methods described in this book, great! But remember that by holding onto any of my Soul Travel methods or anyone else's, you'll likely be retarding your own progress. Once you get started as a Soul Traveler, break away and develop out-of-body techniques better suited for you personally. By experimenting with various different Soul Travel methods that you dream up yourself, with persistence and perseverance you should be able to eventually develop techniques of your own that work fairly well for you.

37

Five Years Later: A Spiritual Fall?

Each chapter of this book has been painfully slow and difficult writing for me, mainly because I'm not a writer, just a person with an important story to tell. This chapter will be even tougher for me because this is one I don't want to write. Basically I'm a rather private person and don't enjoy revealing my own inner feelings, faults, and limitations. In this chapter I'm going to have to say some things about myself that I'd just as soon my friends and family members didn't have to read. However, I can't justify leaving this part of my story out, so here goes.

Today, a little more than five years since my first conscious out-of-body experience, it's become much easier for me to consciously leave my body. The bad news is that my spiritual progress has slipped dramatically over the past couple of years. The past two years have provided me with a wealth of Soul Travel knowledge and experience. But for me there's no question about my recent loss of spiritual growth; it clearly shows in my attitude toward myself and other people.

Two years ago my Soul Travel life and adventures were my first priority in life. This showed in my attitude of giving goodwill to other people and not caring so much about my own vanity. Recently, however, I became strangely preoccupied with my appearance, especially concerned about a long, rather wicked-looking scar that runs across my forehead. Improving my appearance became my number one priority. Following close behind was concern over my financial situation and job. How could my Soul Travel and spiritual priorities have slipped so far behind? My physical life had become most important, at the expense of my inner travels.

Maybe it's a natural state of affairs, but because of this, I don't see the Inner Master nearly as often during my inner travels anymore, and the hole on top of my inner body head has closed up. Two years ago I was having lots of conscious out-of-body experiences with the Inner Master, but not so today; nowadays my face-to-face inner encounters with the Inner Master are only occasional. The closing of the hole on top of my inner body head happened gradually over a period of about six months when my interest in Soul Travel slipped behind my desire to have my forehead scar fixed. I also felt a lessening in the stream of energy that used to flow into the top of my head through this opening, my overall out-of-body conscious awareness declined somewhat, and I started having less success delaying automatic returns to my physical body.

I'm just hanging in there now as best I can, struggling along, hoping for the best. What the end result will be of my scar operations and how well I mentally accept the end result remains to be seen, but one thing is for certain. Until I'm able to forget about myself and my appearance, and begin pointing my attention selflessly outward toward other people, I don't know if I'll be able to start back up the spiritual ladder again. Spiritual growth is reflected in attitude, not Soul Travel ability; it begins with forgetting or disregarding personal ego and turning the attention away from the personal self, something that's easier said than done.

38

Two Easier Ways to Soul Travel

My present-day out-of-body awareness isn't as good on the average as it was a couple of years ago, and my out-of-body travels with good conscious awareness are shorter now on the average than they used to be. But one big area of improvement in my Soul Travel ability has been the gradual shortening of my contemplation sessions.

Two years ago my middle-of-the-night contemplations often exceeded two hours, but nowadays my nighttime contemplations rarely last over an hour and a half. They are usually from thirty minutes to an hour, and my odds of moving out of the body are still good, maybe two out of three. As in the past, nearly all my travels are to inner life-like worlds rather than the physical environment.

At the present time I'm using two particular contemplation methods with good success, one of which I've already described. I'll probably always be experimenting with different contemplation patterns, searching for easier ways to consciously leave my body, but here are descriptions of the techniques I'm relying on now. The steps prior to contemplation are still the same as those described in chapter 32.

Contemplation Technique G
The first is a simplified combination of several different

contemplative techniques which have been effective for me in the past.

I try in this technique to point my attention in two directions. I mentally induce a slight tingling sensation or feeling of tightness at the spot just in back of the top center of my head.

Then I'll split my attention in a second direction by gradually relaxing the muscles of my eyelids. This is how I try to drift into sleep. The key to this Soul Travel technique's success is to keep a slight tingling sensation or feeling of tightness at that certain spot on top the head, but just as important, is keeping the eyelids and eyelid muscles fully relaxed. Usually when using this technique I'll drift unsuspectingly into sleep with very good chances of becoming conscious during sleep of already being out of the body in an inner world. Keeping the eyelids and eyelid muscles fully relaxed while contemplating serves several important purposes in this technique, including drawing the black inner screen close to the inner viewpoint, and nullifying the effect of the emotions of fear and anticipation.

My advice to you if you happen to be considering trying this Soul Travel method is this: (1) Expect to do some experimenting to be able to mentally induce that slight tingling sensation or feeling of tightness near the top center of your head. (2) Don't be concerned or frustrated if your mind wanders constantly during contemplation; just keep trying and keep your attention focused as best you can. (3) Don't expect to feel yourself leave your physical body if this Soul Travel method works for you; more than likely you'll shift automatically into some inner-world dimension during an early stage of sleep and then suddenly become conscious or partially conscious of what's happening and what you're doing. (4) Don't expect to have full out-of-body conscious awareness; you may have, but you may not.

The other contemplative technique that I sometimes use today is the chanting method described earlier in this book (as contemplative technique E in chapter 35). Most nights

I'll chant like this for a few minutes at bedtime before going to sleep, and sometimes I'll use this contemplative technique in the middle of the night, when my chances of moving out of the body automatically with conscious awareness are usually pretty good.

Conscious out-of-body experiences still seem to come to me in bunches, and this pattern has pretty much held true since early in my Soul Travel career. Today my nighttime contemplations will reward me with a string of neat Soul Travel adventures for a week or two, but then, as I become more nonchalant about them, my conscious experiences become fewer and fewer. Eventually after a lean Soul Travel period of maybe two weeks, I'll get serious again about contemplating at nights and my Soul Travel success will return.

I mention this pattern because others may notice a similar pattern in their Soul Travel adventures, too.

39

A Confession

I've spent years writing this book, trying as best I can to word it in a way that sounds believable and hopefully gives you the notion that you or anyone else can consciously experience and verify the reality of out-of-body travel. Now I'm going to twist this next-to-last chapter in a direction that will probably surprise you. Breaking all rules of persuasive writing, I'm going to make the statement here that even if you do have the desire to try to experience a conscious out-of-body sensation, I don't give you very good odds of succeeding. For every twenty people wanting to consciously experience what I've spoken of in this book, my guess is that maybe only one person will eventually succeed. I don't make this statement to discourage you, only because I believe it to be true.

Supposing you are an individual who's come to believe after reading this book that maybe I am telling the truth about Soul Travel. Maybe now you'd like to consciously experience and verify what I'm talking about. All people have the same latent Soul Travel capabilities. Soul Travel is a learned ability much like playing football or driving a car. The more a person does it, the easier it gets. Then what could possibly hold you back? Being a believer or non-believer in the possibility of Soul Travel won't make much difference in your out-of-body success. Desire isn't even the most crucial factor in Soul Travel success, although people with the greatest desire to experience out-of-body travel will naturally have the best chances for success because of being willing to persevere longer.

My reason for giving you such poor odds of success can be attributed to one word — time. Time, patience, and desire are the three requirements for out-of-body success, and of these three, time is by far the most elusive. The fast pace of today's living, especially here in the western world, just doesn't leave most people with much free time; my one and only possible advantage over other people in getting started as a Soul Traveler has been my free time.

A good friend of mine back in Iowa grew up with a strong interest and belief in all things of psychic and supernatural nature. She had heard about Eckankar and Soul Travel many years before I did, but so far she's been unable to achieve that first conscious trip out of the body and declares now that she's given up. This young lady's problem isn't due to a lack of belief or desire; her stumbling block is time. She's a wife and mother, and she has a full-time job. She just doesn't have much free time to donate toward trying various Soul Travel techniques. And her situation is typical of many other people.

Please don't misunderstand what I'm trying to say here. There's nothing wrong with being a busy person or leading a busy life. There's nothing at all wrong with this or any other lifestyle; being married, having children, and having a good enjoyable job can offer rewards of love and satisfaction that can't be priced. All I'm saying here is that unfortunately today's fast pace of living keeps a big percentage of the population on the go much of the time, loading people down with stress and robbing people of free time.

To those of you who do manage to achieve that first conscious out-of-body experience, who persevere and make the time to do it, even with the poor odds of success I've given you, my congratulations will certainly be a very small part of your reward. One conscious experience out of the body can give you proof that there is life after death, and that nonphysical worlds do exist. Walk into any church anywhere in the world and ask any number of preachers if there's life after death, and most will say they believe in an afterlife. But few of these people will really know. There's a big difference between believing and knowing, between having faith and knowing, between accepting other people's say-so and knowing. The knower doesn't have to argue or debate over the question because the knower just simply knows! Just one conscious trip out of the body can transform anyone, a believer or nonbeliever, into a knower. Becoming a knower about the afterlife exposes death for what it really is, merely a transition from life in one world to life in another.

I remember several years ago traveling by shuttle bus from the St. Louis airport to downtown to catch my next job on a riverboat. A conversation got started between another passenger and a group of about six priests who were also on the bus. After some small talk the passenger asked the priests about the afterlife, what life would be like for him after he died and what he would consist of. His sincere questions to the priests drew nothing but a couple of short quotes from the Bible and a solemn assurance that there is life after death.

I couldn't help thinking at the time how typical this man's questions were; most people throughout the world would dearly love to know the answers to these same questions. What this fellow and most other people don't realize, however, is that Soul Travel can unlock the answers to all questions about the afterlife. The commonly accepted notion that a person has to wait until death to find out what's next simply isn't true. Science and religions may not be able to agree on what awaits each of us after death, but even the beginning Soul Traveler can start sorting out important

173

answers to various questions about the afterlife, questions considered intangible and unprovable by most people.

40

Beyond Soul Travel

I 'd like to leave you with a final thought, before closing this book and retiring my writing pen. I've spoken
so admirably about Soul Travel throughout this book, but
from what I've read and now accept to be true, the phenomenon of out-of-body travel is far from the ultimate in
spiritual experience and spiritual attainment.

Out-of-body travel can help a person begin climbing the
spiritual ladder toward the goal of God-Consciousness and
is an important first step. But once a person's consciousness
has been expanded and he begins reaching into the inner
worlds of pure Spirit, worlds beyond the realm of time,
space, and matter, out-of-body travel then becomes unnecessary.

Most people believe that their lives are directed by the
outer conscious mind. They think that it controls thought
and behavior rather like a master computer. The few individuals who've elevated themselves spiritually to a level
known as Self-Realization understand that the conscious
and subconscious minds both begin to subordinate to the
direction of Soul, which is really in the driver's seat. The
Self-Realized person begins thinking and acting more and
more according to the spiritual direction of Soul, instead of
to the whims and desires of the conscious mind. The person

can unfold to spiritual heights, receiving from God a greater and greater current of Light and Sound (Spirit) which enters into the physical body and the inner bodies through the top of the head, like an ever-stronger current of energy.

My reason for pointing this book specifically toward out-of-body travel instead of more lofty spiritual goals is that Soul Travel is an excellent starting place for spiritual growth. It is also something tangible that all people can consciously experience and get excited about. Lofty spiritual goals can seem so unrealistic and unreachable to most people, but out-of-body travel is a provable phenomenon that can spark a person to begin developing his or her latent Soul Travel abilities and begin considering the existence of God and Spirit and Soul.

Soul Travel can nudge a person toward taking a greater interest in the spiritual side of life, to the realization that there is a process of spiritual learning and purification going on here in the physical world as well as in the inner worlds.

ECKANKAR Also Offers Spiritual Study Courses

People want to know the secrets of life and death. In response to this need Sri Harold Klemp, today's spiritual leader of Eckankar, and Paul Twitchell, its modern-day founder, have written special monthly discourses which reveal the Spiritual Exercises of ECK—to lead Soul in a direct way to God.

Those who wish to study Eckankar can receive these special monthly discourses which give clear, simple instructions for the spiritual exercises. The first two annual series of discourses are called *Soul Travel 1—The Illuminated Way* and *The ECK Dream Discourses.* Mailed each month, the discourses are designed to lead the individual to the Light and Sound of God.

The techniques in these discourses, when practiced twenty minutes a day, are likely to prove survival beyond death. Many have used them as a direct route to Self-Realization, where one learns his mission in life. The next stage, God Consciousness, is the joyful state wherein Soul becomes the spiritual traveler, an agent for God. The underlying principle one learns is this: Soul exists because God loves It.

Study of the ECKANKAR discourses includes:

(1) Twelve monthly discourse lessons (Some titles from the series *Soul Travel 1—The Illuminated Way:* "The Law of Strength," "Love as a Doorway to Heaven," "The Universality of Soul Travel," and "The Spiritual Cities of This World." From *The ECK Dream Discourses:* "Dreams—The Bridge to Heaven" and "The Dream Master.")

(2) The *Mystic World,* a quarterly newsletter with articles about Spirit and a special Wisdom Note and feature article by today's Living ECK Master, Sri Harold Klemp.

(3) Special mailings to keep you informed of upcoming seminars and activities around the world, new study materials, tapes from Eckankar, and more.

How to find out more about the monthly ECKANKAR discourses

For more information on how to receive these discourses, use the coupon at the back of this book. Or during business hours, call (612) 544-0066, weekdays. Or write: ECKANKAR, Att: ECK Study, P.O. Box 27300, Minneapolis, MN 55427 U.S.A.

There May Be an
ECKANKAR Study Group near You

Eckankar offers a variety of local and international activities for the spiritual seeker. With over three hundred study groups worldwide, Eckankar is near you! Many cities have Eckankar Centers where you can browse through the books in a quiet, unpressured environment, talk with others who share an interest in this ancient teaching, and attend beginning discussion classes on the spiritual principles of ECK.

Around the world, Eckankar study groups offer special one-day or weekend seminars on the basic teachings of Eckankar. **Check your phone book under ECKANKAR, or write ECKANKAR, Att: Information, P.O. Box 27300, Minneapolis, MN 55427 U.S.A. for the Eckankar Center or study group nearest you.**

☐ Please send me information on the nearest Eckankar discussion or study group in my area.

☐ I would like an application form for the twelve-month Eckankar study discourses on the innermost secrets of Soul Travel and spiritual unfoldment.

Please type or print clearly   941

Name _____

Street _____ Apt. # _____

City _____ State/Prov. _____

Zip/Postal Code _____ Country _____

(Our policy: Your name and address are held in strict confidence. We do not rent or sell our mailing lists. Nor will anyone call on you. Our purpose is only to show people the ECK way home to God.)

ECKANKAR
Att: Information
P.O. Box 27300
Minneapolis, MN 55427
U.S.A.